ILLUSTRATED LIBRARY OF COOKING

VOLUME **9** Fru-Hol

A five-star volume, Volume 9!
To begin it: Fruits around
the Calendar with dozens of
luscious fruit desserts and
salads. Next, a special section
on Garnishes. Third: a primer
of Herbs and Spices that
includes recipes for old-
fashioned sachets and
pomanders. Fourth: the latest
on Nutrition and fifth, a whole
year's worth of holiday feasts.

ROCKVILLE HOUSE PUBLISHERS, INC.
ROCKVILLE CENTRE, NEW YORK 11570

Family Circle®

Illustrated Library of

COOKING

YOUR READY REFERENCE FOR A LIFETIME OF GOOD EATING

Picture Credits:
Jean Anderson • California Strawberry Advisory Board • The Chocolate Information Council • George Nordhausen • Pacific Kitchen • Photo Courtesy of Motts

Chefette Fruit Plate

Table of Contents

Nectarines aren't hybrids but smooth-skinned peaches. They're an ancient fruit that predates Christianity.

Grapes are a great American favorite, for eating out of hand as well as for making salads and desserts.

1030

Three favorite American fruits, cantaloupe, honeydew melon and sweet red cherries team up for dessert.

FRUITS AROUND THE

CALENDAR

FRUITS AROUND THE CALENDAR:
SPRING AND SUMMER FAVORITES,
FALL AND WINTER FAVORITES,
YEAR-ROUND TROPICAL FAVORITES,
TROPICAL EXOTICS

Eve's apple just may have been a pear (or so some historians now think). Anyhow, that's just one of many fascinating legends about fruits. Another: To dream of raspberries betokens a long and happy marriage. And another: To cure gout, eat strawberries.

Most fruits have had a long and lively history. Delightful reading. What concerns us here, however, is not the past but the present. The *eating,* not the reading. Fruits as they come to us each season, fruits as they're enjoyed day to day, as they're used in recipes.

Modern farming, packaging and transportation have literally put the world of fruits at local supermarkets. Fruits still do come and go with the seasons, it's true, but that merely makes them more enjoyable. In this section, the individual fruits are discussed by season: Spring and Summer Favorites (all the marvelous berries and melons, not to mention peaches and apricots) . . . Fall and Winter Favorites (apples and pears, to name two) . . . Year-Round Tropical Favorites (the whole sunny citrus family, bananas, pineapples). Shopping and storage tips are included for each fruit as well as FAMILY CIRCLE'S very best recipes.

SPRING AND SUMMER FAVORITES

SOME GENERAL FRUIT-SHOPPING TIPS:

Buy in season when both fruits and prices are the best.
Buy only what fruits you can use up within a short period of time. Fruits are perishable.
Reject damaged fruits, even if the price is cut-rate.
Handle fruit carefully in the store—it bruises easily.
Buy mature, fully ripe fruits of good color and aroma; reject those showing bruises, blemishes, mold or decay.
Don't be carried away by size. The biggest fruit is *not* always the best.
Look for USDA GRADES on fruits. The U.S. Department of Agriculture has established grade standards for most fresh fruits (whether or not a packer uses these grades is voluntary). But grades do frequently appear on fresh fruits and are an indication of quality: The top grade is U.S. FANCY or U.S. No. 1.

Fruit	SPRING AND SUMMER FAVORITES	
	Season	Shopping Tips
APRICOTS	June and July	Look for plump, juicy apricots of uniform orange-gold color.
BLUEBERRIES	May through September	Choose firm, deep-blue berries with silvery bloom.
CHERRIES (SWEET)	May through August	Select dark, rich red fruits—it's your best guarantee of ripeness *and* sweetness. *Note:* Most sour cherries are sold frozen or canned.
MELONS	Varies with variety. See *A Closer Look at Melons,* which follows and also includes Shopping Tips.	
NECTARINES	June through September	These are smooth-skinned peaches. Choose those of rich peach-to-rose color, those that are plump and beginning to soften along the seam.
PEACHES	July to September	There are two main types—*freestone* (flesh does not cling to pit) and *clingstone* (flesh *does* cling to pit; these are "canning" peaches).
PLUMS	June to September	Choose firm-soft, fragrant fruits of rich red-to-purple or blue color.
RASPBERRIES, BLACKBERRIES, BOY-SENBERRIES, DEW-BERRIES	July to September	These differ as to color, size and flavor, but structurally, they're the same. Regardless of species, look for clean bright berries, unbroken, unmoldy with no attached stem caps.
STRAWBERRIES	April to July	Look for rich red berries, plump and firm with cap stems still attached.

APRICOTS

1032

Apricot Rice-Pudding Pie
Creamy rice pudding plus juicy golden apricots add up to a double dessert-treat.
Bake at 400° for 30 minutes. Makes one 9-inch pie

½ cup uncooked regular rice
½ cup sugar
2 tablespoons butter or margarine
¼ teaspoon salt
¼ teaspoon ground allspice
1 cup milk
1 cup water
1 package piecrust mix

1 can (1 pound, 13 ounces) apricot halves, drained
Cream
Sugar

1 Combine rice, sugar, butter or margarine, salt, allspice, milk and water in large saucepan; heat to boiling. Cover; simmer 30 minutes, or until rice is tender but still moist. Remove from heat; save for next step.
2 Prepare piecrust mix, following label directions, or make pastry from your favorite two-crust recipe. Roll out half to a 12-inch round on lightly floured pastry cloth or board; fit into a 9-inch pie plate. Spoon rice mixture into shell; arrange apricot halves, rounded side up, on top.
3 Roll out remaining pastry to a rectangle, 12x8;

A trio of spring and summer fruits—honey-sweet, vine-ripened watermelon cut in fat chunks and sharing a crisp pie shell, mellow apricots and blueberries.

brush lightly with cream and sprinkle with sugar; cut into 10 strips, each about ¾ inch wide. Weave strips over filling to make a crisscross top; trim overhang to ½ inch; turn up over edge and flute.

4 Bake in hot oven (400°) 30 minutes, or until pastry is golden. Cool on wire rack. Serve with cream or a dollop of creamy topping from a pressurized can, if you wish.

Honeyed Fruit Kebabs
For a taste you'll be glad you acquired, try broiling ripe fruit on skewers.
Makes 6 servings

3 large firm ripe pears

3 large firm ripe apricots
3 medium-size apples
3 medium-size firm ripe bananas
½ cup (1 stick) butter or margarine
2 tablespoons brown sugar
1 tablespoon honey
2 teaspoons lemon juice
1 teaspoon ground ginger
¾ teaspoon ground cinnamon
½ teaspoon ground mace

1 Pare pears, quarter and core; peel apricots, pit and quarter; quarter apples and core; cut each piece of fruit in half. Peel bananas; cut each crosswise into six pieces.
2 Thread all fruits, dividing evenly, onto six long skewers. Place on rack in broiler pan.

3 Melt butter or margarine in a small saucepan; stir in brown sugar, honey, lemon juice and spices; brush part of mixture over fruits.

4 Broil, 4 to 6 inches from heat, turning and brushing several times with remaining honey mixture, 10 minutes, or until lightly glazed. Serve hot with baked ham or chicken or veal curry.

BLUEBERRIES

Blueberry Cheesecake Glacé
Bake at 325° for 1 hour and 25 minutes, then leave in oven 1 hour with heat off. Makes 12 servings

1½ cups graham cracker crumbs
1¼ cups sugar
  4 tablespoons (½ stick) butter or margarine, melted
  3 packages (8 ounces each) cream cheese, softened
  4 eggs
  2 cups (16-ounce carton) dairy sour cream
  1 cup cream for whipping
  1 teaspoon grated lemon peel
½ teaspoon vanilla
  1 jar (10 ounces) currant jelly
  1 tablespoon water
1½ cups blueberries, washed and stemmed

1 Combine graham cracker crumbs with ¼ cup of the sugar in a medium-size bowl; blend in melted butter or margarine. Press evenly over bottom and side of a buttered 9-inch spring-form pan. Chill while making filling.

2 Beat cream cheese until smooth in a large bowl; slowly beat in remaining 1 cup sugar until creamy-smooth.

3 Beat in eggs, one at a time; stir in sour cream, cream for whipping, lemon peel and vanilla. Pour into prepared crust.

4 Bake in slow oven (325°) 1 hour and 25 minutes; turn off heat. Leave cake in oven, with door closed, 1 hour longer. Remove from oven. Cool completely in pan on a wire rack. (Cake will settle slightly as it cools.)

5 Loosen cake around edge with a knife; re-

Luscious summer line-up: Blueberry Cheesecake Glacé, (left), Cantaloupe Cream Melba (center top), Honeydew Horn of Plenty (right) and (front) a fresh peach pie.

lease spring and carefully lift off side of pan. Slide cake, still on metal base, onto a serving plate.

6 Combine currant jelly with water in a small saucepan. Heat slowly, stirring constantly, until jelly melts; remove from heat; cool slightly.

7 Spread blueberries over top of cheesecake; spoon cooled jelly mixture over blueberries. Chill at least a half hour, or until glaze sets. Just before serving, garnish top and bottom edges of cake with rings of whipped cream, and additional blueberries, if you wish.

Blueberries

Blueberry Streusel Puffs
Bake at 400° for 25 minutes. Makes 1 dozen

1½ cups sifted all-purpose flour
2 teaspoons baking powder
½ teaspoon salt
4 tablespoons (½ stick) butter or margarine
½ cup sugar
1 egg
1 teaspoon vanilla
½ cup milk
1 cup blueberries, washed and stemmed
STREUSEL-WALNUT TOPPING (recipe follows)

1 Sift flour, baking powder and salt onto wax paper.
2 Cream butter or margarine with sugar until fluffy-light in a large bowl; beat in egg and vanilla. Stir in flour mixture, alternately with milk; fold in blueberries.
3 Place a paper baking cup in each of 12 large muffin-pan cups. Spoon batter into cups, filling

1036

each about half full; sprinkle with STREUSEL-WALNUT TOPPING.

4 Bake in hot oven (400°) 25 minutes, or until tops spring back when pressed with fingertip. Remove from pans; cool on a wire rack.

STREUSEL-WALNUT TOPPING—Melt 2 tablespoons butter or margarine in a small saucepan; remove from heat. Stir in 2 tablespoons brown sugar, ¼ teaspoon ground cinnamon and ¼ cup chopped walnuts.

Mandarin Blueberry Pie
Bake at 400° for 45 minutes. Makes one 9-inch pie

4 cups (2 pints) blueberries, washed and stemmed
1 jar (about 11 ounces) mandarin-orange segments, well drained
1 cup sugar
3 tablespoons quick-cooking tapioca
¼ teaspoon salt
¼ teaspoon ground cinnamon
1 package piecrust mix
2 tablespoons butter or margarine
1 tablespoon cream
Cinnamon-sugar

1 Combine blueberries and orange segments in a large bowl; sprinkle with sugar, tapioca, salt and cinnamon; toss to mix well.
2 Prepare piecrust mix, following label directions, or make pastry from your favorite two-crust recipe. Roll out half to a 13-inch round on a lightly floured pastry cloth or board; fit into a deep 9-inch pie plate; trim overhang to ½ inch.
3 Spoon fruit mixture into shell; dot with butter or margarine.
4 Roll out remaining pastry to an 11-inch round; cut several slits near center to let steam escape; place over filled shell. Trim overhang to ½ inch; turn edges under together, flush with rim; flute edge. Brush top crust with cream; sprinkle lightly with cinnamon-sugar
5 Bake in hot oven (400°) 45 minutes, or until pastry is golden and juices bubble up. Cool at least two hours on a wire rack before cutting. Serve plain, or topped with scoops of vanilla ice cream, if you wish.

Summer Fruit Tart
Dewy-fresh blueberries and golden apricots top a layer of pineapple cream.
Bake at 400° for 15 minutes. Makes one 10-inch tart

Tart Shell

1 package piecrust mix
2 tablespoons sugar
¼ teaspoon ground cardamom
1 egg, slightly beaten

Filling

1 cup (8 ounces) cream-style cottage cheese
1 cup milk
1 package (3¾ ounces) pineapple-cream flavor instant pudding mix
1 can (1 pound, 13 ounces) apricot halves, drained
2 cups blueberries, washed, stemmed and drained

Glaze

¼ cup sugar
1 tablespoon cornstarch
½ cup apricot syrup (from can)
1 tablespoon lemon juice

1 Make tart shell: Combine piecrust mix, sugar and cardamom in medium-size bowl; stir in egg with a fork, mixing lightly just until dough holds together.
2 Roll out to a 13-inch round on lightly floured pastry cloth or board; fit into a 10-inch pie plate. Trim overhang to ½ inch; turn under flush with rim; flute edge; prick all over with a fork.
3 Bake in hot oven (400°) 15 minutes, or until golden; cool completely on wire rack.
4 Make filling: Combine cottage cheese and milk in medium-size bowl; stir in instant pudding mix; continue stirring 1 minute, or until mixture begins to thicken. (It will be slightly lumpy.) Pour into cooled tart shell; chill.
5 Arrange apricot halves and blueberries in quarter sections on top of filling.
6 Make glaze: Combine sugar and cornstarch in small saucepan; stir in apricot syrup. Cook, stirring constantly, until sauce thickens and boils 3 minutes; remove from heat; stir in lemon juice. Spoon hot glaze over filling; chill.

CHERRIES

Cherries Jubilee
Makes 6 servings

2 teaspoons cornstarch
1 tablespoon sugar
1 can (1 pound) pitted black bing cherries

Flaming Cherries Jubilee will light up any dinner.

2 strips orange peel
1 strip lemon peel
⅓ cup warm cognac
1 quart vanilla ice cream

1 Mix cornstarch and sugar in a medium-size saucepan. Drain 1 cup syrup from the can of cherries and stir into cornstarch mixture. Drop in orange and lemon peels. Cook, stirring constantly, over moderate heat until sauce thickens and boils 3 minutes. Discard peels and add cherries.
2 Transfer to a chafing dish and carry to the dining table. Add warm cognac and blaze with a match.
3 Ladle flaming over bowls of vanilla ice cream.

A CLOSER LOOK AT MELONS

Learning to identify each kind of melon and its quality marks is smart buymanship. Tips here will help you.

Cantaloupes and watermelons are the most popular members of the melon family. Peak season runs from about June through September, but thanks to modern-day methods of growing and shipping, it's getting longer every year. Other varieties once thought of as luxuries, are popular-priced today and show up in supermarkets from summer through late fall and on into the holiday season.

What's in a Melon?
Besides plain elegant eating, melons are good for you, for they're packed with vitamins. And what a boon to weight-watchers! Half a medium-size cantaloupe = 25 calories; quarter of a small honeydew = 50 calories; a slice of sugary-sweet watermelon about ¾ inch thick and 6 inches across = 100 calories.

1038

When You Shop for Melons:
Depending on variety, there's a size to fit every need. Most melons are sold whole, either by size or weight. One exception is watermelon, which also comes in halves, quarters, and slices—usually priced by the pound. Cantaloupes, particularly, are perfect for two to four

servings. And while some honeydews are small enough for four servings, most belong in the bigger class with Cranshaws, Persians, and casabas. For top flavor, cantaloupes and watermelon must ripen on the vine; other kinds ripen nicely in your kitchen, so it pays to know how to judge a good melon.

How to Store Melons at Home:
If the melon is ripe when you buy it, rinse off and dry well, and place in a plastic bag or wrap, to keep the flavor in the melon and out of other foods. Then store in the refrigerator. If your choice (other than cantaloupe or watermelon) is not quite ripe, keep it at room temperature for a day or two until it reaches the best-eating stage, then rinse, wrap, and chill. Once cut, melon should always be carefully wrapped to protect its flavor.

Hints on Serving Melons:
Use melon as soon as possible after cutting, as it loses flavor quickly. Most fans agree that it tastes its sweetest if served just cold—not icy cold—so set it out at room temperature about an hour before cutting. Served plain or with a sprinkling of salt or lemon or lime juice, almost any melon makes a perfect treat from breakfast eye-opener through dinner top-off. But don't miss out on the inviting combination dishes you can make too. Just a few examples:

• Cut almost any variety into balls or cubes and pour fizzy ginger ale over for a sparkling appetizer or dessert cup.
• Cut up, mix with other colorful fruits and mold into shimmery gelatin for salad-dessert.
• Slice honeydew into crescents to star in cold platters and fruit plates, or wrap with paper-thin slices of ham for an appetizer.
• Slice honeydew or cantaloupe into rings and fill with cottage cheese, fruit or sherbet for a refreshing salad or dessert.
• Heap cantaloupe halves with vanilla ice cream or raspberry sherbet for an **à la mode** favorite.

HOW TO PICK A GOOD MELON

Cantaloupe—Most popular of all melons and easily recognized by its ribbed oval shape, green-yellow skin almost covered with a raised coarse netting, and pinkish-orange sweet meat. Check the stem end, as vine-ripened cantaloupe shows a sunken smooth scar—not a bit of stem—where it was clipped from the vine. This

For Party Melon Tray, make honeydew basket, till with Avocado Chip Cream, ring with melon balls and slices.

scar, heavy netting on skin, and sweet aroma are your best buying guides. You'll find varying sizes from May to November.

Honeydew—Large creamy-yellow melon, bluntly oval in shape and weighing from four to six pounds. Its color, smooth velvety skin, slight softness at the blossom end and pleasant odor are your tips for ripeness. When cut, honeydew has delicate green, sweet, very juicy meat. Its big season is June through October.

Persian—A large round melon, weighing as much as 8 pounds, with a deep-green rind very evenly covered with a fine netting. Similar to a cantaloupe, its meat is deep orange-pink, with a mildly sweet, very pleasant flavor. Season runs from July to October.

Cranshaw—One of our newer melons, and some think the sweetest-tasting of them all. Pointed at the stem end and round at the base, it has fairly smooth golden-green skin. Meat is salmon-color, very juicy and slightly spicy. As this melon ripens, its golden yellow color deepens. Season is July to October, so enjoy this prize often.

FRUITS AROUND THE CALENDAR

Casaba—Another large, roundish melon, sometimes pointed at its stem end. The rind has deep furrows with no netting, and when ripe, its color is deep butter-yellow. Unlike most melons, a casaba has almost no fragrance, but the meat is soft, creamy-white and meltingly juicy with a sweet delicate flavor. Season is July to December.

Watermelon—This family is a big one, both in variety and size, and weights may go as high as 40 pounds. These two varieties are most popular: (1) The big roundish melon with very dark green skin and crisp pink meat. And (2) the supersize oblong melon with handsome gray-green to dark green irregularly striped skin. Its meat, too, is pink, sweet and crisp. When you buy a whole watermelon, look for a symmetrical shape with fresh deep-green skin that looks thin enough to scratch easily with a fingernail. Or better still, let your produce man guide you, as he knows best what is ripe.

Watermelon Ice
Makes 4 servings

3 cups small pieces watermelon, seeded
2 tablespoons lemon juice
½ cup sugar
1 envelope unflavored gelatin
½ cup water

1 Place watermelon, about half at a time, in an electric-blender container; cover. Beat until smooth and liquid. (There should be about 2 cups.) Pour into a medium-size bowl; stir in lemon juice. (If you do not have a blender, press watermelon through a sieve into a bowl.)
2 Mix sugar and gelatin in a small saucepan; stir in water. Heat slowly, stirring constantly, until gelatin dissolves. Cool slightly; stir into watermelon mixture. Pour into a pan, 9x9x2.
3 Freeze about 1½ hours, or until firm around edges.

Great buffet stunt: fill a huge watermelon basket with your favorite fresh fruit combination.

4 Spoon into a large bowl; beat until smooth; return to pan. Freeze several hours longer, or until firm.

Cantaloupe Cream Melba
Makes 8 servings

1 package (10 ounces) frozen raspberries, thawed
⅔ cup sugar
Dash cream of tartar
1 large cantaloupe
1 quart peach or vanilla ice cream

1 Press raspberries through a sieve into a small saucepan; stir in sugar and cream of tartar.
2 Heat quickly, stirring constantly, to boiling; cook 3 minutes. Pour into a small bowl; chill.
3 Halve cantaloupe; scoop out seeds; pare melon. Cut each half into 4 wedges.
4 Arrange wedges, spoke fashion and rounded sides down, around edge in a compote or shallow serving bowl; scoop ice cream into balls and pile in center. Drizzle part of the raspberry sauce over ice cream, then serve remainder separately.

Honeydew Horn of Plenty
Makes 6 servings

2 medium-size honeydew melons
¼ large watermelon
1 can (6 ounces) frozen concentrate for orange juice, thawed
½ cup dry white wine
3 limes

1 Halve one of the honeydew melons; scoop out seeds. Cut out enough balls with a melon-ball cutter or the ½ teaspoon of a measuring-spoon set to make 3 cups; place in a medium-size bowl. Remove seeds from watermelon; cut into balls. (There should be about 3 cups.) Combine with honeydew balls.
2 Pour the orange-juice concentrate and wine over fruit in bowl; toss lightly to mix; cover. Chill at least 4 hours to blend flavors.
3 Just before serving, cut a thin slice diagonally from end of remaining honeydew melon; scoop out seeds with a long-handle spoon. Make a ½-inch-deep cut all around melon just inside rind with a small sharp-tip knife.
4 Slice limes thin; quarter each slice. Push part of the wedges, rind side out, into cut in melon.

5 Place melon at one end of a large serving plate; spoon chilled melon balls into hollow and along plate to resemble a cornucopia. Garnish with remaining lime wedges, and orange wedges, if you wish.

Carolina Melon Salad
Makes 6 to 8 servings

6 cups broken salad greens
1 small cantaloupe, pared, seeded and sliced thin
½ small honeydew melon, pared, seeded and sliced thin
1 lime, sliced thin
GINGER DRESSING (recipe follows)

1 Partly fill a large salad bowl with greens; arrange slices of cantaloupe, honeydew and lime, overlapping, in rings on top.
2 Serve with GINGER DRESSING to spoon over. Or layer the melon slices with salad greens in bowl. Drizzle about ¼ cup dressing over; toss to mix and coat greens well. Serve with lime slices. (Save remaining dressing for salad for another meal.)
   GINGER DRESSING—Combine ½ cup olive oil or vegetable oil, ¼ cup wine vinegar or cider vinegar, 1 teaspoon sugar, 1 teaspoon celery salt, ½ teaspoon ground ginger, and ¼ teaspoon salt in jar with tight-fitting lid; shake well to mix. Makes about ¾ cup.

Buffet Melon Basket Salad
Makes 16 servings

½ small watermelon (crosswise cut)
1 cantaloupe, halved and seeded
½ small honeydew melon, seeded
1 large honeydew melon, halved lengthwise, seeded and cut into 16 crescents
Fresh mint
ORANGE-CREAM DRESSING (recipe follows)

1 Trim a 1-inch-thick round from cut end of watermelon. Make balls of pink meat with a melon-ball scoop or half teaspoon of a metal measuring-spoon set. Place in a small bowl and save for next step. Trim any remaining meat close to rind, leaving circle of rind whole; save circle for base of "basket" in Step 3.
2 Cut out about 3 cups of balls from remaining watermelon and add to bowl. Cut 2 cups balls

1041

from cantaloupe, and 1 cup from the half honeydew. Place in separate bowls; cover; chill until serving time.

3 When ready to serve, place saved circle of rind on a large serving plate. Stand honeydew crescents around inside of circle, so lower ends meet in the center and rind rests against watermelon circle. (Hold ends in place with one hand while putting remaining crescents in place with the other.)

4 Carefully spoon watermelon balls into bottom of basket. Top with layers of cantaloupe and honeydew balls. Garnish with a few sprigs of fresh mint. Serve with ORANGE-CREAM DRESSING.

●

Orange-Cream Dressing
Makes 2 cups

½ cup sugar
1 teaspoon flour
½ teaspoon dry mustard
¼ teaspoon salt
2 eggs
½ cup orange juice
⅓ cup lemon juice
½ cup cream for whipping

1 Mix sugar, flour, mustard and salt in a cup.

2 Beat eggs slightly in top of a double boiler; blend in dry ingredients, then stir in orange and lemon juices.

3 Cook, stirring constantly, over simmering water, 5 minutes, or until mixture coats a metal spoon. Remove from heat; strain into a medium-size bowl; cover. Chill.

4 Just before serving beat cream until stiff in a small bowl; fold into chilled dressing.

●

Party Watermelon Bowl
A trick with a cookie cutter turns watermelon into a pretty server for ham-chicken salad.
Makes 6 servings

1 five-inch piece of watermelon, cut from an end
2 cups diced cooked ham
2 cups diced cooked chicken
2 cups sliced celery
2 tablespoons sweet-pickle relish
1 teaspoon salt
½ cup mayonnaise or salad dressing
½ cup dairy sour cream

More melon magic: Party Melon Bowl (rear), Buffet Melon Basket Salad (right), Cantaloupe Fruit Coupe (front).

1 Place watermelon on a cutting board; trim off rounded end to make bottom flat. Make scallops around top this way: With a 2-inch cookie cutter, cut scallops about ½ inch apart through green skin and white rind to pink meat. Run a sharp knife between rind and meat to separate; lift out cut pieces of rind.

2 Cut a guideline around top in pink meat 1 inch in from green skin. Working inside guideline, cut out about 24 balls with a melon-ball scoop or the half teaspoon of a metal measuring-spoon set to form a shallow bowl. Place balls in a small bowl; cover and chill along with watermelon bowl.

3 Combine ham, chicken, celery, sweet-pickle relish and salt in a medium-size bowl; fold in mayonnaise or salad dressing and sour cream; cover; chill.

4 When ready to serve, place watermelon bowl on a large serving plate. Pile ham-chicken salad in center; circle with watermelon balls; top with 3 or 4 more balls.

Note—After serving, cut off top of watermelon bowl and discard. Slice remaining melon as fruit for another meal.

Cantaloupe-Fruit Coupe
Makes 6 servings

3 small ripe cantaloupes
2 cups strawberries (1 pint)
2 cups sliced peaches
1 can (about 13 ounces) frozen pineapple chunks, thawed and drained
1 can (8 ounces) apricot halves, drained
2 bananas, peeled and sliced
½ cup toasted slivered almonds (from a 5-ounce can)
HONEY DRESSING *(recipe follows)*
10X (confectioners' powdered) sugar

1 Mark a guideline lengthwise around middle of each cantaloupe with tip of knife, then make even saw-tooth cuts into melon above and below line all the way around. Pull halves apart gently; scoop out seeds.

2 Set aside 6 of the prettiest strawberries for next step; slice remaining and combine with peaches, pineapple, apricots, bananas and almonds in a medium-size bowl; fold in HONEY DRESSING.

3 Spoon fruit mixture into cantaloupe halves. Dip tips of saved whole strawberries into 10X sugar; place 1 on top of each salad.

HONEY DRESSING—Combine ¼ cup vegetable oil, 2 tablespoons lemon juice, 1 tablespoon honey, ¼ teaspoon salt and ⅛ teaspoon ground ginger in a jar with tight-fitting lid; shake well to mix; chill. Makes about ½ cup.

Frosted Honeydew Crescents
Makes 8 servings

1 can (1 pound, 13 ounces) fruit cocktail
1 package (3 ounces) strawberry-flavor gelatin
1 cup hot water
2 tablespoons lemon juice
1 package (8 ounces) cream cheese
½ cup mayonnaise or salad dressing
1½ cups tiny marshmallows
½ cup sliced maraschino cherries
½ cup cream for whipping
1 honeydew melon

1 Drain syrup from fruit cocktail into a 2-cup measure to use in next step. Set fruit aside for Step 3.

2 Dissolve gelatin in hot water in a small bowl; stir in 1¼ cups syrup and lemon juice; cool to lukewarm.

3 Soften cream cheese in a large bowl; blend in mayonnaise or salad dressing, then lukewarm gelatin mixture. Fold in fruit cocktail, marshmallows and cherries.

4 Beat cream until stiff in small bowl.

5 Place bowl of fruit-gelatin mixture in a larger bowl or pan partly filled with ice and water; fold in whipped cream. Continue folding, keeping over ice, 10 minutes, or until mixture starts to mound lightly on a spoon.

6 Pour into 2 ice-cube trays or an 8-cup shallow pan. Freeze 3 hours, or until firm.

7 When ready to serve, cut honeydew into 8 wedges; remove seeds; place wedges on serving plates. Spoon a mound of frozen fruit mixture onto each wedge. (Keep any remaining fruit mixture frozen to serve on lettuce for another meal.)

Sunshine Fruit Salad
Makes 6 servings

4 cups broken salad greens
3 cups mixed cantaloupe and honeydew-melon balls
2 oranges, peeled and sectioned
3 thin slices Bermuda onion, separated into rings

¼ cup vegetable oil
2 tablespoons cider vinegar
½ teaspoon sugar
¼ teaspoon salt
¼ teaspoon dillweed
⅛ teaspoon dry mustard
⅛ teaspoon paprika

1 Partly fill a salad bowl with greens; top with melon balls, orange sections and onion rings.
2 Combine remaining ingredients in a jar with tight-fitting lid; shake well.
3 Drizzle half over salad; toss lightly to mix. Pass remaining dressing.

Party Melon Tray
Makes 8 servings

2 small honeydew melons
¼ watermelon
2 limes, sliced thin
1 medium-size cantaloupe
AVOCADO CHIP CREAM (recipe follows)

1 Make honeydew basket this way: Mark a guideline lengthwise around center of one of the melons with the tip of a knife, then mark off an inch-wide strip across top for basket handle. Cut out sections between marks; remove seeds from "basket" and sections, then chill both until ready to arrange tray.
2 Cut 16 balls from watermelon with a small ice-cream scoop or tablespoon of a measuring-spoon set; remove seeds. Cut about a dozen tiny balls from remaining watermelon with a melon-ball scoop or ¼ teaspoon of a measuring-spoon set; chill all.
3 When ready to serve, thread tiny watermelon balls and lime slices on wooden picks; stick into handle of basket. Set basket in center of a large tray.
4 Halve remaining honeydew melon and cantaloupe; remove seeds; slice melons and saved honeydew sections into thin wedges. Arrange around basket on tray. Stack big watermelon balls in a pyramid in front. Spoon AVOCADO CHIP CREAM into basket.

Avocado Chip Cream
Makes about 2½ cups

1 large ripe avocado
1 package (8 ounces) cream cheese

½ cup dairy sour cream
2 tablespoons lemon juice
2 tablespoons honey

1 Halve avocado, then peel and pit. Cut one half into small chunks and place in an electric-blender container. Slice in cream cheese, then add sour cream, lemon juice and honey; cover. Beat at high speed 1 minute, or until smooth. (If you don't have a blender, mash avocado in a medium-size bowl, then beat in remaining ingredients until smooth.)
2 Cut remaining half of avocado into ¼-inch cubes; fold into dressing; cover; chill.

NECTARINES

Nectarine Pie
Cook's guide: Two pounds of fruit, sliced, will make about 4 cups.
Bake at 425° for 45 minutes. Makes one 9-inch pie

1 package piecrust mix
4 cups sliced pared nectarines
½ cup granulated sugar
¼ cup firmly packed brown sugar
¼ cup sifted all-purpose flour
1 teaspoon grated lemon peel
¼ teaspoon ground cinnamon
⅛ teaspoon salt
1 teaspoon lemon juice
2 tablespoons butter or margarine
1 tablespoon milk or cream

1 Prepare piecrust mix, following label directions, or make pastry from your own favorite two-crust recipe. Roll out half to a 12-inch round on a lightly floured pastry cloth or board; fit into a 9-inch pie plate; trim overhang to ½ inch.
2 Place nectarines in a large bowl. Sprinkle with granulated and brown sugars, flour, lemon peel, cinnamon, salt and lemon juice; toss lightly to mix. Spoon into prepared pastry shell; dot with butter or margarine.
3 Roll out remaining pastry to an 11-inch round; cut several small designs in crust with a knife; remove cutouts; place crust over pie. Trim overhang to ½ inch; turn edges under, flush with rim; flute edge all around. Brush top with milk or cream; arrange cutouts on crust; brush cutouts.

1045

4 Bake in hot oven (425°) 45 minutes, or until pastry is golden and juices bubble up. Cool pie on a wire rack. Serve plain or with cream.

Nectarine Cup Custards
Bake at 325° for 50 minutes. Makes 8 servings

    4 cups very thinly sliced pared nectarines
    3 eggs
    3 tablespoons sugar
    ⅛ teaspoon salt
    1 teaspoon vanilla
    3 cups milk, scalded

1 Divide nectarine slices among eight 6-ounce custard cups.
2 Beat eggs slightly in a 4-cup measure; stir in sugar, salt, and vanilla; slowly stir in scalded milk. Strain over nectarines in cups, dividing evenly.
3 Place cups in a shallow baking pan on oven shelf; pour boiling water into pan to depth of about an inch.
4 Bake in slow oven (325°) 50 minutes, or until centers are almost set but still soft. (Do not overbake, as custard will set as it cools.) Remove cups from water at once. Serve warm or chilled.

PEACHES

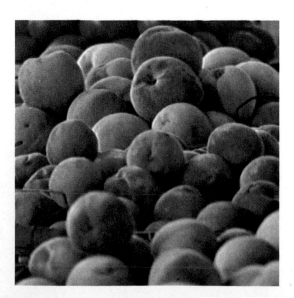

Georgia Peach Torte
Bake shell at 375° for 20 minutes. Makes 8 servings

      1 cup sifted all-purpose flour
      ¼ cup sugar
      6 tablespoons (¾ stick) butter or margarine
      1 egg yolk
      2 packages (about 3 ounces each) coconut-cream–flavor pudding mix
      2 cups milk
      4 medium-size firm ripe peaches
    1½ teaspoons cornstarch
      2 tablespoons light corn syrup
    1½ teaspoons lemon juice
    1½ cups cream for whipping
      1 teaspoon vanilla
        Pecan halves

1 Sift flour and sugar into a medium-size bowl; cut in butter or margarine with a pastry blender until mixture is crumbly. Stir in egg yolk until pastry holds together and leaves side of bowl clean, then knead several minutes, or until very smooth. Press into bottom and up side of a 9-inch spring-form pan to make a 1½-inch-high shell. (Do not prick.)
2 Bake in moderate oven (375°) 20 minutes, or until golden. Cool completely in pan on a wire rack.
3 Blend pudding mix and milk in a medium-size saucepan; cook, following label directions. (Pudding will be thick.) Pour into a large bowl; cover surface with transparent wrap; chill well.
4 While pudding chills, peel peaches, halve and pit. Place in a single layer in a medium-size frying pan; add water to cover. Heat to boiling; simmer 2 minutes. Measure 6 tablespoons of the liquid into a small saucepan, then drain off remaining; set peaches aside to cool.
5 Blend cornstarch slowly into saved liquid; stir in corn syrup. Cook, stirring constantly, until mixture thickens and boils 1 minute, remove from heat; stir in lemon juice.
6 Beat cream with vanilla until stiff in a medium-size bowl; fold, a small amount at a time, into thickened pudding until thoroughly blended; spoon into cooled pastry shell. Arrange peach halves, rounded side up, in ring on top; spoon glaze over peaches. Garnish with pecan halves. Chill several hours, or until firm.
7 When ready to serve, remove torte from pan; cut into wedges.

Just peachy! (Left to right) Peach Angel Pie, Georgia Peach Torte and creamy Frozen Peach Soufflé-ettes.

PEACHY TRICKS WITH PEACHES

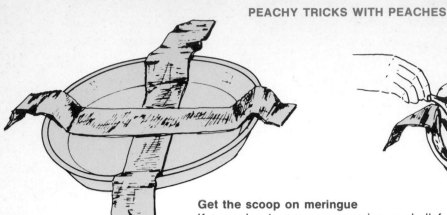

Get the scoop on meringue

If you plan to remove a meringue shell from its baker for serving, place strips of foil in the pie plate first. Then as the shell is loosened, use the strips as a lifter to keep it from breaking.

To shape shell: Spoon meringue into plate and, working from center, push it up the side into peaks.

Soaring success

A paper collar helps an individual frozen soufflé hold its head handsomely high, and can be fitted ever so easily onto a demitasse or custard cup. To make, cut a double-thick strip of foil and wrap around cup to stand two inches above rim, molding at handle if there is one. Fasten with paper clip and rubber band.

Smooth way to peel a peach

The secret is to hold the peach on a spoon and dip it into hot water for about a minute, then into cold water to cool it quickly. Break skin with a small sharp-tip knife and slip it off—almost like magic!

1048

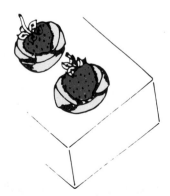

Give peaches a buildup

Berry-bright—that's how this pretty garnish looks atop a cake, pie or shortcake. To fix it, overlap peach slices in a ring, stacking them two layers high. Nestle a plump strawberry, stem end up, in the center.

Flute a peach
Starting at the center of a plump peach half, make even curved cuts about ⅛ inch deep to edge. Then make a second cut right behind each line, slanting knife in just a bit. Lift out the narrow strip; top peach with a whole clove.

Simple artistry
No talent needed, as it's the arrangement that counts here. Place peach crescents, rounded side out and close together in rings. *Presto*—a pretty scallop trim.

● ● ●

Peach Praline Pie
Bake at 450° for 10 minutes, then at 350° for 20 minutes. Makes one 9-inch pie

  4 *cups sliced peeled peaches*
   (about 2 pounds)
¾ *cup granulated sugar*
2 *tablespoons quick-cooking tapioca*
1 *package piecrust mix*
½ *cup sifted all-purpose flour*
¼ *cup firmly packed brown sugar*
4 *tablespoons (½ stick) butter or margarine*
½ *cup chopped pecans*

1 Mix peaches, granulated sugar and tapioca in a large bowl; let stand while preparing pastry.
2 Prepare piecrust mix, following label directions, or make pastry from your own favorite one-crust recipe. Roll out to 12-inch round on lightly floured pastry cloth or board; fit into a 9-inch pie plate. Trim overhang to ½ inch; turn under, flush with rim; flute.
3 Combine flour and brown sugar in a small bowl; cut in butter or margarine with pastry blender until mixture is crumbly; stir in pecans.
4 Sprinkle ⅓ over bottom of pastry shell; top with peach mixture; sprinkle remaining pecan mixture over.
5 Bake in very hot oven (450°) 10 minutes. Lower heat to moderate (350°); bake 20 minutes longer, or until peaches are tender and topping

is golden. Cool on wire rack before cutting. Serve warm or chilled.

●

Peach Angel Pie
Bake at 275° for 1 hour. Makes 8 servings

 5 *eggs*
¼ *teaspoon cream of tartar*
¼ *teaspoon salt*
1⅔ *cups sugar*
¼ *cup lemon juice*
½ *cup cream for whipping*
4 *medium-size firm ripe peaches, peeled and sliced*

1 Crisscross two strips of foil, each 15x2, in a 9-inch pie plate, leaving a 2-inch overhang on each end. Coat pie plate and strips generously with butter or margarine; dust lightly with flour, tapping out any excess. (Foil strips make it easy to remove baked meringue from pie plate, if you wish.)
2 Separate 4 of the eggs, placing whites in a large bowl and yolks and remaining whole egg in the top of a medium-size double boiler for Step 4. Add cream of tartar and salt to egg whites; beat until foamy-white and double in volume; sprinkle in 1 cup of the sugar, 1 tablespoon at a time, beating all the time until sugar dissolves completely and meringue stands in

1049

firm peaks. (Beating will take about 25 minutes in all with an electric beater.) Spoon into prepared pie plate, building up side and dishing center slightly to make a shell.

3 Bake in very slow oven (275°) 1 hour, or until pale golden; cool completely in pie plate on a wire rack.

4 Add remaining ⅔ cup sugar and lemon juice to egg yolks in top of double boiler; beat slightly. Cook, stirring constantly, over simmering water, 10 minutes, or until mixture thickens slightly and coats a metal spoon; strain into a medium-size bowl; cool completely.

5 Beat cream until stiff in a small bowl; fold into custard mixture.

6 To remove meringue shell from pie plate, run a knife gently around edge to loosen completely, lifting up on foil strips at the same time. Lift shell out; peel off foil; place shell on a serving plate.

7 Arrange sliced peaches around edge in shell; spoon custard mixture in center. Chill at least 2 hours, or until filling is softly set. Just before serving, garnish with more peach slices. Cut into wedges.

Peach Streusel Cream Cake
Bake at 350° for 50 minutes. Makes 12 servings

    2 cups sifted all-purpose flour
 1½ teaspoons baking powder
    ½ teaspoon baking soda
    ½ teaspoon salt
    1 cup (2 sticks) butter or margarine
 1½ cups sugar
    2 eggs
    1 cup (8-ounce carton) dairy sour cream
    2 teaspoons grated orange peel
    1 teaspoon vanilla
    1 teaspoon cinnamon
    ¾ cup finely chopped walnuts
    6 medium-size firm ripe peaches, peeled and sliced
 1½ cups cream for whipping
    2 tablespoons 10X (confectioners' powdered) sugar

1 Grease 2 baking pans, 9x9x2. Line each with a sheet of foil long enough to fit across bottom and up two sides with a 1-inch overhang; grease foil; dust lightly with flour, tapping out any excess.

2 Sift flour, baking powder, soda and salt onto wax paper.

3 Cream butter or margarine with 1¼ cups of the sugar until fluffy in a large bowl; beat in eggs, 1 at a time, then sour cream; stir in orange

1050

peel and vanilla. Stir in flour mixture, a third at a time, blending well after each addition.

4 Mix remaining ¼ cup sugar, cinnamon and walnuts in a small bowl.

5 Spread about ¼ of the batter into each prepared pan; sprinkle each with ¼ of the sugar-walnut mixture, then top with remaining batter, dividing evenly. Arrange peach slices in rows on top; sprinkle with remaining sugar-walnut mixture.

6 Bake in moderate oven (350°) 50 minutes, or until a wooden pick inserted into tops comes out clean. Cool layers in pans on wire racks 10 minutes, then remove by lifting up on foil strips; cool completely; peel off foil.

7 When ready to serve, beat cream with 10X sugar until stiff in a medium-size bowl. Stack layers on a serving plate, shortcake style and peach sides up, with cream between and on top.

Frozen Peach Soufflé-ettes
Makes 12 servings

    4 medium-size firm ripe peaches, peeled and cut up
 1⅔ cups sugar
    4 eggs, separated
    ¼ teaspoons cream of tartar
    ⅓ cup water
    1 teaspoon vanilla
    1 cup cream for whipping

1 Prepare 12 freezerproof demitasses or small parfait glasses this way: Cut strips of foil twice the depth of cups or glasses and long enough to wrap around each with a 1-inch overlap; cut out notches to fit around cup handles. Wrap each strip around a cup or glass to make a 2-inch stand-up collar; hold in place with a rubber band and a paper clip.

2 Beat peaches until puréed in an electric blender (or mash, then press through a sieve); place in top of a medium-size double boiler; stir in 1 cup of the sugar and egg yolks. (Set remaining ⅔ cup sugar aside for Step 4.)

3 Cook peach mixture, stirring constantly, over simmering water 10 minutes, or until it thickens slightly and coats a metal spoon; remove from heat. Cool completely for Step 6.

4 Combine remaining ⅔ cup sugar with cream of tartar and water in a small saucepan. Heat slowly, stirring constantly, until sugar dissolves, then cook rapidly, *without stirring*, to 236° on a candy thermometer. (A spoonful of syrup will form a soft ball when dropped in cold water.)

5 While syrup cooks, beat egg whites until they form soft peaks in a large bowl; *gradually pour in hot syrup in a thin stream,* beating constantly, until meringue stands in firm peaks; beat in vanilla.

6 Beat cream until stiff in a medium-size bowl. Fold cooled peach custard, then whipped cream into meringue until no streaks of white remain. Carefully spoon into prepared demitasses or parfait glasses. Freeze several hours, or until firm. (Overnight is even better.)

7 When ready to serve, carefully peel off foil collars; garnish each dessert with whipped cream and peach slices, if you wish.

PLUMS

Royal Fruit Tart

Here's a luscious way to butter up both fruit- and cream-pie fans at once.

Bake at 400° for 20 minutes. Makes one 9-inch tart

1 package piecrust mix
2 tablespoons sugar
1 egg
1 package (about 4 ounces) vanilla-flavor pudding mix
⅛ teaspoon ground nutmeg

1 cup milk
1 small can evaporated milk (⅔ cup)
1 teaspoon vanilla
1 can (about 1 pound) sliced cling peaches
1 tablespoon cornstarch
1 tablespoon lemon juice
1 can (1 pound, 14 ounces) whole purple plums, drained and pitted

1 Combine piecrust mix, sugar and egg in medium-size bowl. Mix with a fork until well blended.

2 Press in bottom and up side of a 9x1½-inch layer-cake pan, making rim flush with edge of pan. (Shell will be thick.) Prick well all over with a fork.

3 Bake in hot oven (400°) 20 minutes, or until golden. Cool on wire rack 10 minutes; carefully invert onto second wire rack; lift off pan. Turn shell right side up; cool completely.

4 Combine pudding mix, nutmeg, milk and evaporated milk in small saucepan. Cook, following label directions; stir in vanilla. Pour into small bowl; cover; chill.

5 Drain and measure syrup from peaches to make ¾ cup. Stir a little into cornstarch until smooth in small saucepan, then add remaining. Cook, stirring constantly, until mixture thickens and boils 3 minutes; stir in lemon juice. Remove from heat, but keep warm.

6 Pour chilled pudding mixture into cooled shell; arrange peach slices and whole plums on top. Spoon warm glaze over. Chill at least 2 hours.

Royal Fruit Tart teams canned cling peaches and canned whole purple plums with pudding and piecrust mixes.

FRUITS AROUND THE CALENDAR

Pinwheel Plum Cobbler
Bake at 400° for 50 minutes. Makes 8 servings

- 10 large plums, halved, pitted and sliced
- 2 medium-size apples, pared, quartered, cored and sliced
- 2¼ cups sugar
- ½ cup sifted all-purpose flour
  Dash of ground cardamom
- 1 package refrigerated crescent rolls
- 2 teaspoons grated lemon peel

1 Combine fruits in a 12-cup baking dish. Sprinkle with 2 cups of the sugar, flour and cardamom; toss to mix well; cover.
2 Bake in hot oven (400°) 30 minutes, or until bubbly around edge.
3 While fruits cook, separate crescent rolls into 4 rectangles. Mix remaining ¼ cup sugar and lemon peel in a cup; sprinkle over rectangles. Roll up, jelly-roll fashion; cut each into 4 slices. Arrange on top of hot fruit mixture.
4 Bake 20 minutes longer, or until biscuits are golden. Serve warm, with ice cream, if you wish.

Plum Compote
Makes 6 servings

- ¾ cup granulated sugar
- 1 cup water
- 3 one-inch pieces stick cinnamon
- 18 large plums, quartered and pitted
- 1 teaspoon grated orange peel

Coconut drifted, liqueur spiked Plum Compote.

3 seedless oranges, pared and sectioned
¼ cup Grand Marnier liqueur
½ cup flaked coconut

1 Combine sugar, water and cinnamon in a large frying pan; heat to boiling. Add plums; simmer 2 minutes, or until plums are tender but still firm enough to hold their shape. Cool; remove cinnamon sticks.
2 Fold in orange peel and sections and Grand Marnier; spoon into a shallow serving bowl. Chill at least an hour.
3 Just before serving, sprinkle with coconut. Garnish with a whole plum cut into a flower shape, if you wish.

RASPBERRIES, BLACKBERRIES, BOYSENBERRIES, DEWBERRIES AND STRAWBERRIES

Berries-and-Cream Crown
Makes 6 servings

1 package (6 ounces) lemon-flavor gelatin
2 cups hot water
½ cup cold water
1 pint raspberries (2 cups)
1 pint strawberry or raspberry ice cream

1 Dissolve gelatin in hot water in a medium-size bowl. Pour ½ cup into a 1-cup measure and stir in cold water, then pour about ¼ cup into a 6-cup mold.
2 Place mold in a pan of ice and water to speed setting. Keep remaining gelatin in bowl at room temperature.
3 Chill layer in mold 20 minutes, or until syrupy-thick.
4 While layer chills, wash raspberries. Arrange 6 whole berries in a ring in gelatin in mold; spoon 2 tablespoons more gelatin mixture from cup over berries; chill until sticky-firm, then spoon remaining gelatin mixture in cup over top. Chill again until sticky-firm.
5 Stir ice cream, a big spoonful at a time, into cooled gelatin in bowl; fold in remaining berries; spoon over sticky-firm layer in mold. Remove from ice and water; chill in refrigerator several hours, or until firm.
6 When ready to serve, run a sharp-tip, thin-blade knife around top of mold to loosen; dip mold *very quickly* in and out of a pan of hot water. Cover mold with a serving plate; turn upside down, then gently lift off mold. Garnish with whole raspberries, if you wish.

Continental Berry Cream
Makes 8 servings

1 package (8 ounces) cream cheese
4 tablespoons (½ stick) butter or margarine
⅓ cup 10X (confectioners' powdered) sugar
2 tablespoons cream for whipping
1 tablespoon lemon juice
¼ teaspoon vanilla
¼ cup finely chopped toasted slivered almonds (from a 5-ounce can)
2 tablespoons finely chopped citron
1 pint raspberries, washed
1 pint blackberries or dewberries, washed

1 Cut a double-thick piece of cheesecloth large enough to line a 2-cup mold and hang over edge slightly; wring out in cold water; line mold.
2 Blend cream cheese and butter or margarine until smooth in a medium-size bowl; beat in 10X sugar until fluffy, then cream, lemon juice and vanilla; fold in almonds and citron.
3 Spoon into prepared mold, smoothing top even, then fold cheesecloth up over top; chill overnight.
4 When ready to serve, pull up on cheesecloth to loosen mold around edge, then turn upside down into a shallow bowl; lift off mold and peel off cheesecloth.
5 Pile raspberries and blackberries or dewberries around cheese mold in bowl.

Fruit Sampler
Makes 4 servings

1 small head of leaf lettuce
2 oranges, peeled and sliced crosswise
2 pears, pared and sliced
2 nectarines, sliced
2 large plums, halved and pitted
½ cup boysenberries, washed
2 tablespoons sugar
⅛ teaspoon ground ginger
CAMEMBERT CREAM (recipe follows)

1 Line 4 salad plates with lettuce.
2 Arrange orange, pear and nectarine slices in separate mounds around edge of each plate,

1053

dividing evenly. Place a plum half in middle, hollow side up; mound berries on top.

3 Mix sugar and ginger in a small cup; sprinkle over fruits; chill. Serve with CAMEMBERT CREAM.

CAMEMBERT CREAM—Mash 2 wedges (1⅓ ounces each) Camembert cheese with fork in small bowl; slowly blend in ¼ cup heavy cream. Makes ¾ cup.

Strawberries Chantilly
Makes 4 servings

    4 egg yolks
    4 tablespoons sugar
      Dash of salt
    ½ cup milk
    ½ cup light cream or table cream
    1 tablespoon rum flavoring
    2 pints (4 cups) strawberries, washed and
      hulled
      10X (confectioners' powdered) sugar

1 Beat egg yolks with sugar and salt until light in top of small double boiler. Stir in milk and cream.

2 Cook, stirring constantly, over simmering water, 8 minutes, or until mixture thickens and coats a metal spoon. Strain at once into a medium-size bowl; stir in rum flavoring; cool.

3 When ready to serve, spoon strawberries into sherbet or dessert dishes, dividing evenly. Pour sauce around strawberries; sprinkle lightly with 10X sugar.

Strawberry-Chiffon Tarts
Bake at 425° for 15 minutes. Makes 12 tarts

    1 package piecrust mix
    1 envelope unflavored gelatin
    ½ cup sugar
    ½ cup water
    1 cup crushed strawberries (about 1 pint
      whole)
    1 tablespoon lemon juice
    1 cup cream for whipping

1 Prepare piecrust mix, following label directions.

2 Roll out half of pastry to ⅛-inch thickness on lightly floured pastry cloth or board; cut out six 6-inch rounds. Fit each into a four-inch tart-shell pan, pressing dough firmly against

1054

(L. to r.) Strawberries Chantilly, Strawberry-Chiffon Tart, Strawberries Parisienne, Strawberry Glacé Surprise.

bottom and side; prick all over with a fork. Repeat with remaining half of pastry.

3 Bake in hot oven (425°) 15 minutes, or until golden; cool completely on wire rack before removing from pans.

4 Combine gelatin and sugar in small saucepan; stir in water. Heat slowly, stirring constantly, 5 minutes, or until gelatin dissolves. Pour over crushed strawberries and lemon juice in medium size bowl; chill until mixture is as thick as unbeaten egg whites.

5 While gelatin mixture chills, beat cream until stiff in small bowl.

6 Place bowl of thickened gelatin mixture in pan of ice and water; beat until fluffy. Fold in whipped cream until no streaks of white remain, then continue folding *just* until mixture mounds. Remove from bowl of ice at once, as mixture is very cold and will set fast.

7 Spoon *quickly* into cooled tart shells, using about 4 tablespoonfuls for each; swirl tops with tip of teaspoon. Chill about 30 minutes. Garnish each with a whole strawberry threaded on a wooden pick, if you wish.

●

Strawberries Parisienne
Makes 6 servings

1 package (3 or 4 ounces) cream cheese
1 cup dairy sour cream
1 tablespoon sugar
¼ teaspoon pumpkin-pie spice
2 cups sweetened sliced strawberries (about 1½ pints whole)

1 Soften cream cheese in small bowl, then beat

1056

until fluffy. Stir in sour cream, sugar and pumpkin-pie spice until well blended.

2 Spoon alternate layers of cream-cheese mixture and strawberries into six parfait or juice glasses, dividing evenly. Garnish each with a sprig of fresh mint, if you like.

●

Strawberry Glacé Surprise
Bake at 250° for 40 minutes. Makes 12 servings

Meringue Shells
3 egg whites
½ teaspoon cream of tartar
⅛ teaspoon salt
1 cup sugar
½ teaspoon vanilla

Filling
¾ cup sugar
3 tablespoons cornstarch
¼ teaspoon salt
3 egg yolks (from meringue shells)
⅓ cup lemon juice
1¼ cups water
1 teaspoon grated lemon peel
2 tablespoons butter or margarine

Glaze
½ cup strawberry jam
½ cup light corn syrup
2 drops red food coloring
4 cups strawberries, washed and hulled (2 pints)

1 Make meringue shells: Beat egg whites, cream of tartar, and salt until foamy-white and double in volume in medium-size bowl. Beat in sugar, 1 tablespoon at a time, beating well after each, until meringue stands in firm peaks. (Sugar should be completely dissolved before adding more. Beating should take about 10 minutes.) Fold in vanilla.

2 Line a large cookie sheet with brown paper; mark twelve 3-inch circles, 2 inches apart, on paper. Drop meringue, about 4 tablespoonfuls for each, inside circles; spread into rounds with small spatula, building up side of each to form a shell.

3 Bake in very slow oven (250°) 40 minutes, or until crisp. Set cookie sheet on wire rack until meringues cool completely, then remove with spatula. (Shells may be made a day ahead and stored in a container with a tight-fitting cover.)

4 Make filling: Combine sugar, cornstarch and salt in medium-size saucepan. Beat egg yolks slightly in 2-cup measure; stir in lemon juice and water; stir into sugar mixture.

5 Cook over medium heat, stirring constantly, until mixture thickens and boils 3 minutes. Remove from heat; stir in lemon peel and butter or margarine; cool.

6 When ready to fill shells, make glaze: Combine jam, corn syrup and red food coloring in small saucepan; heat, stirring constantly, just until hot; remove from heat.

7 To fill shells, spoon about 2 tablespoons filling into each; top with 6 whole strawberries, standing each tip end up; spoon about 1 tablespoon warm glaze over. (Shells may be filled about an hour before serving time, if you like, then chilled.)

●

Coeur à la Crème with Fresh Strawberries

A gourmet French dessert, traditionally eaten with crisp crackers.
Makes 6 servings

1 package (8 ounces) cream cheese
1 cup (8 ounces) cottage cheese
1 cup cream for whipping
2 teaspoons 10X (confectioners' powdered) sugar
  Pinch of salt
3 cups unhulled strawberries, washed
  Crisp soda crackers

1 Let cream cheese soften in medium-size bowl at room temperature; put cottage cheese through sieve into same bowl; gradually blend in cream, 10X sugar and salt until creamy-smooth; chill 1 hour.

2 Line six individual heart-shape molds with wet double-thick cheesecloth; pack with cheese mixture; fold edges of cloth over tops; turn molds upside down on a wire rack set in a shallow pan to catch any liquid; chill overnight.

3 Unmold onto serving plates; remove cheesecloth; serve surrounded with whole or cut strawberries and crisp crackers.

●

Strawberry Cream Tower Glacé

Homemade creamy ice cream packed into a tall mold, then turned out and framed with candied berries, makes this dazzle.
Makes 8 to 10 servings

2 eggs
¾ cup sugar
⅛ teaspoon salt
2 cups cream for whipping
¾ cup milk
1 teaspoon vanilla

Both high and handsome: Strawberry Cream Tower Glacé.

3 cups (1½ pints) strawberries, washed, hulled
  and crushed
  CANDIED STRAWBERRIES (recipe follows)

1 Beat eggs with sugar and salt until blended in large bowl; stir in cream, milk, vanilla and strawberries.
2 Pour into 8-cup can of electric or hand-crank ice-cream freezer; freeze, following manufacturer's directions.
3 Repack ice cream into a 6-cup tall mold or 6-cup deep freezerproof bowl. Freeze overnight or until ready to serve.
4 To unmold, run a long thin-blade knife around side to loosen, then dip mold quickly in and out of a pan of warm water. Invert onto serving plate; lift off mold carefully. Circle base with CANDIED STRAWBERRIES; place another at tip of mold.

Candied Strawberries
Sparkling sugar coating fairly shatters as you bite into each juicy berry.
Makes 2 dozen

24 large strawberries (about 1 pint)
 3 cups sugar
½ cup light corn syrup
½ cup water

1 Pick over strawberries, choosing only perfect ones. (If brusied or cut, their juices will flow and dissolve the candy coating.) Wash, but do not hull; dry on paper toweling. Pull back hulls and insert a wooden pick deep into each.
2 Mix sugar, corn syrup and water in small heavy saucepan; heat, stirring constantly, until sugar dissolves, then cook rapidly, without stirring, to 285° on candy thermometer. (A teaspoon of syrup dropped into cold water will separate into strands that are hard but not brittle.) Remove from heat at once.
3 Working with 1 berry at a time, hold by wooden pick and dip into hot syrup, turning to coat berry completely. (Work quickly. Job is easier if you tip pan slightly so syrup flows to one side.) Lift berry from syrup; let excess drip back into

pan, then turn berry, pointed end up, and hold for 10 seconds, or until syrup hardens.
4 Place on a foil-covered wire rack to cool. Keep berries at room temperature and serve within 2 hours, because syrup cooks them just enough to make juices flow, which will dissolve coating as berries stand.

STRAWBERRIES AND RHUBARB—A HAPPY TWOSOME

Botanically, rhubarb is not a fruit (it belongs, surprisingly, to the buckwheat family), but it is best *treated* like fruit. It teams magnificently with strawberries—both are succulent and sweet, both come to market in the spring.

Strawberry-Rhubarb Shortcake
Bake at 450° for 20 minutes. Makes 8 servings

 1 pound rhubarb
1¾ cups granulated sugar
 2 tablespoons water
 1 pint strawberries (2 cups)
 2 cups sifted all-purpose flour
 3 teaspoons baking powder
½ teaspoon salt
 5 tablespoons butter or margarine
¼ cup vegetable shortening
 1 egg
⅓ cup milk
 1 cup cream for whipping
 2 tablespoons 10X (confectioners' powdered)
   sugar

1 Wash rhubarb, trim ends and cut in 1-inch pieces. (There should be about 3 cups.)
2 Combine with ¾ cup of the granulated sugar and water in a medium-size heavy saucepan; cover. Heat over low heat to boiling, then simmer 5 minutes, or until tender; remove from heat. Set aside to cool. (Rhubarb will finish cooking in heat from pan.)
3 Wash strawberries, hull and slice into a medium-size bowl; sprinkle with ½ cup of the remaining granulated sugar; set aside while making shortcake.
4 Sift flour, remaining ½ cup granulated sugar, baking powder and salt into a medium-size bowl; cut in 4 tablespoons of the butter or margarine and shortening with a pastry blender until mixture is crumbly.
5 Beat egg slightly with milk in a small bowl;

One of spring's happiest couples—scarlet, succulent-sweet stalks of rhubarb and plump, sugary strawberries.

add all at once to flour mixture; stir with a fork until evenly moist. Turn out onto a lightly floured pastry cloth or board; knead gently ½ minute. Pat into a greased 8-inch layer-cake pan.

6 Melt remaining 1 tablespoon butter or margarine in a small frying pan; brush over dough; sprinkle lightly with granulated sugar, if you wish.

7 Bake in very hot oven (450°) 20 minutes, or until golden. Cool in pan on a wire rack 5 minutes; turn out onto rack.

8 Beat cream with 10X sugar until stiff in a medium-size bowl.

9 Split warm shortcake with a sharp knife; place bottom layer on a serving plate. Top with half each of the rhubarb, strawberries and cream; cover with remaining shortcake layer, fruit and cream.

10 Cut into wedges with a sharp knife; serve warm.

●

Two-Fruit Custard Pie
Bake at 400° for 1 hour. Makes one 9-inch pie

  1 *package piecrust mix*
  3 *eggs*
¼ *cup milk*
1¾ *cups sugar*
⅓ *cup sifted all-purpose flour*
  1 *pound rhubarb, washed, trimmed and cut in ½-inch pieces (about 3 cups)*

  1 *cup strawberries, washed, hulled and halved*
  1 *tablespoon butter or margarine*

1 Prepare piecrust mix, following label directions.

2 Roll out half to a 12-inch round on a lightly floured pastry cloth or board; fit into a 9-inch pie plate; trim overhang to ½ inch.

3 Beat eggs slightly with milk in a large bowl; stir in sugar and flour, then rhubarb and strawberries. Spoon into prepared pastry shell; dot with butter or margarine.

4 Roll out remaining pastry to a rectangle, 12x8; cut lengthwise into 10 strips. Weave strips over filling to make a lattice top. Trim overhang to ½ inch; turn under with bottom crust, flush with rim; flute edge.

5 Bake in hot oven (400°) 1 hour, or until pastry is golden and juices bubble up. Cool on a wire rack.

1059

FALL AND WINTER FAVORITES

Fruit	Season	Shopping Tips
APPLES		
CRANBERRIES	*Note:* Each of these fruits, its varieties, seasons and hallmarks of quality is discussed individually in the pages that follow.	
GRAPES		
PEARS		
PUMPKINS		

APPLES

Happily, no one ever seems to tire of this all-American fruit. Notes below, and the chart that follows, will help you know your apples.

How to Buy Your Money's Worth
With their shiny-bright color, apples are their own best display packages. In most supermarkets you'll find them stacked to buy by the piece or pound, in tray packs and in family-size transparent bags. Often the packaged ones are labeled with the kind of apple, its U. S. grade (such as FANCY) and the supermarket brand name—all quality buying helps for you. Learn to recognize a few varieties, so you can pick out the kinds your family likes best and those that best suit your need. Although most of our apple crop comes from just five states, many areas also sell other locally grown specialties. It's smart shopping to watch for them when their seasons are on, for they are often the thriftiest.

Eating vs. Cooking Apples
Tart firm apples are generally referred to as cooking apples, and the sweeter varieties as eating apples, although many kinds are tagged "all-purpose." When you buy, select firm, bright fruit, noticing the size as well as the variety. An apple that's about 2½ inches in diameter is ideal for all-round use. Smaller fruit—usually lower in price—is perfect for turning into sauce and pie, or serving to children; large fruit is best for baking. *Tip:* If you buy just one kind, sort out the beauties for snacktimes, then cook the rest.

What Are "CA" Apples?
In the trade, "CA" apples are those hand-picked at their peak of perfection and stored at once in "controlled-atmosphere" (CA) vaults that literally put the fruit to sleep and keep its fresh-picked flavor and crispness until springtime—formerly an out-of-season appletime. Today only about 10% of the total apple crop is stored in these CA vaults, but more and more of each year's harvest is being marked for them. Naturally we pay more for a handsome red or golden Delicious or a Rome Beauty in June than we do in the fall, when the new apple harvest is in, but the eating pleasure it gives is worth the extra pennies.

THE TOP 7 APPLES

There's no one exact way to pinpoint every variety of apple. But you can learn a few identifying characteristics that will help you spot your favorites quickly.

Delicious—Red or yellow; sweet, and firm; with five points at blossom end. Perfect for eating.

McIntosh—Medium-size; deep red, striped with yellow; tart, juicy. Ideal for cooking and eating raw.

Winesap—Small to medium; deep red, dotted with white; crisp. Good keeper for eating, baking.

1061

A typical American harvest of favorite autumn fruits.

FRUITS AROUND THE CALENDAR

Rome Beauty—Large; greenish-yellow with red stripes; firm, crisp. Ideal for baking, cooking.

Jonathan—Small to medium; rich red, speckled with gold; slightly tart, juicy. Excellent for all uses.

York Imperial—Medium to large; purplish-red over yellow; crisp. Just right for eating, cooking.

Stayman—Medium to large; dull red stripes; firm, juicy. A perfect all-purpose choice.

●

HOW TO STORE APPLES AT HOME

Of all fresh fruits, apples are probably the best keepers and, with a little extra care, they will stay fresh-tasting and firm for several weeks— even months. Here are a few tips for proper storage:

Sort over fruit and take out any with soft spots, skin breaks, or bruises to use immediately. Wash the rest, if it's a small quantity, pat dry and store in a moisture-tight bag in a cold well-ventilated place or in the refrigerator. If left in a warm room, they tend to turn mealy or mushy, develop an overripe flavor, and lose their crispness rapidly.

After sorting, store large quantities—late fall and winter varieties—in baskets in a clean, cold, well-ventilated room. The temperature should be about 35° and the air slightly moist to prevent shriveling. Every so often, check the apples again, removing any that may have developed soft spots.

America leads the world in production of apples. The big apple states: Washington, Michigan, New York.

APPLE DIVIDENDS

An apple a day may keep the doctor away, but canned, bottled, or dried apple products in your cupboard pay off, too, in goodness, convenience, and versatility. A few to consider:

Applesauce—What would we do without this standby, available in just about every size container. Look, too, for the double-fruit treats combining applesauce or chunks of apple with a variety of other fruits.

Apple Juice—This popular breakfast eye-opener simply needs chilling and it's ready to pour. Newest arrival in this category is frozen apple-juice concentrate to mix with water. And for those Halloween treats or a refreshing pickup, tangy apple cider rates a special star.

Apple Slices—Use them right from can or jar in fresh or baked desserts. Stock up, too, on blush-pink spiced rings packed in a jar.

Apple Pie Filling—What a boon to the pie baker, for it's seasoned and ready to go.

Dried Apples—Look for these chewy treats in the dried-fruit section of your supermarket. Most come in boxes or transparent bags, along with suggestions for cooking.

Favorite eating apples include Red and Golden Delicious, McIntosh.

Applesauce
Makes 4 servings

2 pounds tart cooking apples, pared, quartered
  and cored
⅔ cup sugar
½ cup water
  Pinch of ground cinnamon
  Pinch of ground nutmeg

Place all ingredients in a large saucepan and simmer, stirring frequently, about 20 minutes, until mushy. Serve hot or cold, plain or with cream.

Cottage Apple Salad
Makes 6 servings

4 medium-size apples, quartered, cored and
  diced
½ cup golden raisins
½ cup chopped walnuts
1 tablespoon sugar
1 tablespoon lemon juice
¼ cup cream-style cottage cheese
¼ cup dairy sour cream

1 Combine apples, raisins and walnuts in medium-size bowl; sprinkle sugar and lemon juice over; toss lightly.
2 Blend cottage cheese and sour cream in 1-cup measure; spoon over apple mixture; toss lightly to mix.

Apple Salad Cups
Makes 6 servings

6 medium-size red eating apples
  Lemon juice
3 medium-size firm ripe peaches
½ cup thinly sliced celery
½ cup halved red grapes, seeded
½ cup tiny marshmallows
¼ cup coarsely broken walnuts
¼ cup mayonnaise or salad dressing
¼ cup dairy sour cream
1 teaspoon sugar
¼ teaspoon salt
  Chicory or curly endive

1 Cut a ¼-inch-thick slice from stem end of each apple; set aside. Core apples not quite to bottom, then hollow out insides, leaving shells ¼ inch thick. Make deep even sawtooth cuts into apple shells all the way around; lift out cut sections. Brush cut surfaces of apples lightly with lemon juice to prevent darkening.

1063

2 Dice enough of the unpared apple cutouts to make 4-cups; place in a medium-size bowl. (Use all remaining apple pieces to make applesauce.)
3 Peel one of the peaches, pit and dice; add to diced apples with celery, grapes, marshmallows and walnuts.
4 Blend mayonnaise or salad dressing, sour cream, 1 teaspoon lemon juice, sugar and salt in a small bowl. Pour over apple mixture; toss lightly to mix.
5 Place each apple cup on a chicory-lined salad plate; spoon salad mixture into centers.
6 Peel remaining two peaches; pit and slice. Arrange slices around base of each salad.

Perfect Fried Apple Rings
Makes 4 servings

2 *large baking apples*
4 *tablespoons (½ stick) butter or margarine*
Cinnamon-sugar

1 Core apples, but do not pare; cut each in 4 thick rings.
2 Melt butter or margarine in a large frying pan; place apple rings in a single layer in pan.
3 Cook slowly 5 minutes; turn. Cook 5 minutes longer, or until apples are tender and lightly browned. Place on a heated serving platter; sprinkle generously with cinnamon-sugar.

Maple Baked Apples
Bake at 350° about 1 hour. Makes 6 servings

1½ *cups blended maple syrup*
1 *teaspoon grated lemon rind*
2 *tablespoons lemon juice*
½ *teaspoon nutmeg*
2 *tablespoons butter or margarine*
6 *large baking apples*

1 Combine maple syrup, lemon rind and juice, nutmeg and butter or margarine in shallow baking dish; place in cold oven and set temperature at moderate (350°).
2 Wash and core each apple; score skin with sharp knife into 8 sections; pare every other section; place apples in same pan; spoon heated syrup over all.
3 Bake apples in 350° oven, basting often with syrup in pan, 1 hour, or until apples are tender but hold their shape.

Maple Baked Apple, an old favorite with a new flavor.

4 Remove from oven; let apples cool in pan; continue to baste tops with syrup to glaze.

Stuffed Baked Apples
Bake at 350° for 1 hour. Makes 6 servings

6 *large baking apples*
½ *cup firmly packed brown sugar*
½ *cup golden raisins*
½ *teaspoon ground cinnamon*
¾ *cup honey*
½ *cup water*
1 *tablespoon butter or margarine*
1 *teaspoon grated lemon peel*

1 Wash apples and core, then pare about one third of the way down from stem end; stand in a shallow baking dish, 13x9x2.
2 Mix brown sugar, raisins and cinnamon in a small bowl; spoon into centers of apples, packing down well.
3 Combine honey, water, butter or margarine and lemon peel in a small saucepan; heat, stirring constantly, to boiling; pour over apples; cover.
4 Bake in moderate oven (350°), basting often with syrup in dish, 1 hour, or until apples are tender but still firm enough to hold their shape.
5 Cool in dish on a wire rack, spooning syrup over apples often to make a rich glaze.

Other Filling Ideas:
Mince—Substitute ¾ cup prepared mincemeat

1064

(from a 1-pound, 12-ounce jar) for the brown sugar, raisins and cinnamon in above recipe.
Date-Nut—Substitute ½ cup finely chopped dates, ¼ cup finely chopped walnuts, 2 tablespoons sugar and ½ teaspoon nutmeg for the brown sugar, raisins and cinnamon in above recipe.

Apple-Raisin Crisp
Bake at 375° for 45 minutes. Makes 6 servings

    4 medium-size tart cooking apples
    ½ cup raisins
    ¾ cup firmly packed brown sugar
    1 teaspoon cinnamon
    ⅛ teaspoon salt
    ½ cup (1 stick) butter or margarine
    4 cups slightly dry small bread cubes (about
        8 slices)
    ½ cup water

1 Pare, quarter, core and dice apples into a medium-size bowl; mix in raisins, brown sugar, cinnamon and salt.
2 Melt butter or margarine in 6-cup baking dish; stir in bread cubes, tossing lightly. Stir in apple mixture; drizzle water over; cover.
3 Bake in moderate oven (375°) 30 minutes; uncover; bake 15 minutes longer, or until apples are tender and top is browned. Serve warm, plain or with milk, cream or ice cream.

Applesauce Cobbler Cake
Bake at 400° for 35 minutes. Makes 6 servings

    6 tablespoons (¾ stick) butter or margarine
    ⅓ cup firmly packed brown sugar
    ½ cup applesauce
    1 tablespoon corn syrup
    ½ teaspoon cinnamon
    2 cups sifted all-purpose flour
    ¼ cup granulated sugar
    3 teaspoons baking powder
    1 teaspoon salt
    ⅓ cup vegetable shortening
    1 egg
    ½ cup milk

1 Cream butter or margarine with brown sugar until fluffy in small bowl; stir in applesauce, corn syrup and cinnamon until well blended. Set aside for topping in Step 3.
2 Sift flour, granulated sugar, baking powder and salt into medium-size bowl; cut in shortening with pastry blender until mixture is crumbly.
3 Beat egg with milk until blended in small bowl; pour over flour mixture; stir just until blended.

Drop by tablespoonfuls into a greased 9-inch round layer-cake pan. Spoon applesauce topping over dough.
4 Bake in hot oven (400°) 35 minutes, or until cobbler cake starts to pull away from side of pan. Break apart into wedges with two forks. Serve warm with cream, sweetened whipped cream or ice cream, if you wish.

Devonshire Apple Pie
Bake at 350° for 40 minutes. Makes one 9-inch pie

    ½ package piecrust mix
    ¾ cup granulated sugar
    ¾ cup firmly packed brown sugar
    2 tablespoons all-purpose flour (for filling)
    1 teaspoon ground cinnamon
    ¼ teaspoon ground nutmeg

Another new twist for baked apples: meringue crowns.

1 teaspoon lemon juice
¾ cup dairy sour cream
6 medium-size tart cooking apples, pared, quartered, cored and sliced (6 cups)
½ cup sifted all-purpose flour (for topping)
4 tablespoons (½ stick) butter or margarine
  Process Cheddar cheese

1 Prepare piecrust mix, following label directions, or make pastry from your favorite single-crust recipe. Roll out to a 12-inch round on a lightly floured pastry cloth or board; fit into a 9-inch pie plate. Trim overhang to ½ inch; turn edge under, flush with rim; flute to make a stand-up edge. Set trimmings aside.
2 Mix granulated sugar, ¼ cup of the brown sugar, the 2 tablespoons flour, cinnamon, nutmeg, lemon juice and sour cream in a large bowl; stir in apples. Spoon into prepared pastry shell.
3 Mix the ½ cup flour and remaining ½ cup brown sugar in a small bowl; cut in butter or margarine with a pastry blender until mixture is crumbly. Sprinkle over apple filling.
4 Bake in moderate oven (350°) 40 minutes, or until apples are tender and topping is golden. Cool on a wire rack.
5 Reroll pastry trimmings; cut out six small leaf shapes with a knife or truffle cutter. Place on a cookie sheet; prick with a fork. Bake in same oven with pie 10 minutes, or until golden. Cool.
6 Shape three tiny "apples" from cheese; stick a whole clove in each for a stem. Just before serving, arrange a cheese apple between each two pastry leaves on top of pie.

1066

Butterscotch Apple Cake
Bake at 350° for 45 minutes. Makes 12 servings

2 large baking apples
¼ cup red cinnamon candies
  Water
½ cup (1 stick) butter or margarine
1 cup firmly packed light brown sugar
8 maraschino cherries
⅓ cup chopped pecans
1 package yellow cake mix
  Eggs
  Whipped cream

1 Core apples, but do not pare; cut each in 4 thick rings.
2 Combine cinnamon candies and ½ cup water in a large frying pan. Heat, stirring constantly, until candies melt; add apple rings. Simmer, turning once, 3 minutes; remove with a slotted spoon and drain on paper toweling.
3 Melt butter or margarine in a baking pan, 13x9x2; stir in brown sugar. Place apple rings in two rows over sugar mixture; top each with a maraschino cherry; sprinkle pecans between apples.
4 Prepare cake mix with eggs and water, following label directions; pour evenly over apples in pan.
5 Bake in moderate oven (350°) 45 minutes, or until golden and top springs back when lightly pressed with fingertip. Cool in pan on a wire rack 10 minutes. Loosen around edges with a knife; invert onto a large serving plate. Let stand 5 minutes; carefully lift off pan. Serve warm with whipped cream.

Apple Dumplings with Raspberry Sauce
Bake at 425° for 35 minutes. Makes 6 servings

6 medium-size baking apples
4 tablespoons (½ stick) butter or margarine
1 cup firmly packed brown sugar
1 teaspoon ground cinnamon
1 package piecrust mix
1 egg, beaten
  RASPBERRY SAUCE (recipe follows)

1 Pare apples and core.
2 Cream butter or margarine with brown sugar and cinnamon until smooth and pastelike in a small bowl. Spoon into hollows in apples, dividing evenly.
3 Prepare piecrust mix, following label directions, or make pastry from your favorite double-crust recipe; divide into 6 equal parts.
4 Roll out, one at a time, to an 8-inch circle on a lightly floured pastry cloth or board; place

Three elegant desserts (left to right): Apple Dumplings, Butterscotch Apple Cake and Devonshire Apple Pie.

filled apple in center. Press pastry firmly around apple, folding underneath; trim any excess. Place on a cookie sheet; brush with part of the beaten egg.

5 Roll out pastry trimmings to a rectangle ⅛ inch thick; cut into long thin strips with a pastry wheel or knife. Press two strips, crisscross fashion, around each dumpling. (Use any remaining pastry trimmings to make small bows on top, if you wish.) Brush strips with beaten egg.

6 Bake in hot oven (425°) 35 minutes, or until apples are tender and pastry is golden. Remove from cookie sheet to a wire rack; serve warm or cold with RASPBERRY SAUCE.

RASPBERRY SAUCE—Thaw 1 package (10 ounces) frozen red raspberries, following label directions. Mix 1 tablespoon cornstarch and 1 tablespoon sugar in a small saucepan; stir in ⅓ cup water and raspberries and syrup. Cook, stirring constantly, until mixture thickens and boils 3 minutes. Press through a sieve into a small bowl; cool. Makes about 1 cup.

CRANBERRIES

Take advantage of the fresh supply while it lasts; the rest of the year, scan grocery shelves and freezer cabinets for canned sauces and relishes, pour-and-drink juices, baking mixes and a host of other cooking conveniences.

Long before the Pilgrims landed, Indians were using cranberries for medicine and food. Early settlers combed the fruit from the bogs with wooden rake-tooth scoops. Today mechanical pickers harvest an annual crop of about a million and a half barrels. Massachusetts produces the largest supply, although Wisconsin, New Jersey, Washington and Oregon contribute a substantial share. Unlike the wild berries of long ago, today's fruit is cultivated to grow larger, brighter in color and more flavorful.

Tips on Buying Cranberries:
Fresh cranberries come in handy 1-pound transparent bags or neat boxes with a see-through window, so it's easy to pick out the best-looking fruit. Size, shape and color will depend on the variety, but as a general rule choose those that are glossy, firm, plump and red. A light pink color usually means an under-ripe berry.

Tips on Storing Cranberries:
Although cranberries keep longer than most berries, they do need to be stored in the refrigerator. Leave them in their store wrapper and, just before you're ready to cook them, rinse in cold water and remove any stems or bruised fruit. Thrifty tip for year-round eating: During the peak months, (November through January) buy extra berries to freeze—a process as simple as placing the unopened bag or box in the freezer. Come cooking time, wash and pick over the berries—no thawing needed. In fact, if you're chopping or grinding them, the job's easier and faster if the fruit is still frozen. To figure your needs, remember that 1 pound of fruit measures 4 cups and makes about 1 quart of whole-berry or jellied sauce.

Year-Round Dividends:
With today's convenience foods and instants, all of us can enjoy the tart flavor of cranberries a great many ways, any time we like. In planning your family's meals, don't overlook any of these choices:

Sauce—Choose either of two styles—whole-berry or jellied. Both come in 8-ounce cans, just right for small families, and 1-pound sizes. Whole-berry is made the old-fashioned way by simply cooking fresh berries with sugar and water until the skins pop. Jellied sauce calls for double processing—first cooking the berries and straining them, then mixing the purée with sugar and cooking again to a jelly stage.

Whole-berry sauce tastes great right from the can with about any meat; as a topper for ice cream, plain cake or custard; or as a glaze for baked ham. The jellied kind is a pantry-shelf indispensable to slice and cut into fancy shapes for garnishing a salad or meat platter or open-face sandwiches. If you're watching calories, check either the diet section or the regular canned-food section of your supermarket for low-calorie sauces in 12-ounce jars.

Juices—'Way out front in the juice group is cranberry-juice cocktail, made of fruit juice, sugar and water and enriched with vitamin C. It's fine as an eye opener, but remember, too, its versatility as a cooking ingredient. For example, try it as a basting sauce for baked apples, chicken, duck and turkey; as a simmering liquid for pot roast or stew; or as a mixer for punch. It's bottled in 16-, 32-, and 48-ounce sizes. Here, too, you'll find a low-calorie counterpart in pints and quarts.

Other beverages—Available in 32-ounce bottles are two flavor blends—cranberry-apple for example, with vitamin C added.

Relish—Look for two tangy types: Cranberry-orange relish in 14-ounce jars on grocery shelves, and, in some areas, 10-ounce packages in freezer cabinets. Either can be spooned straight from container to serving dish as a meat accompaniment or other bright lift for any meal.

For a Change . . .

Bake a few slices of jellied cranberry sauce along with a ham steak or chicken and serve hot. Unbelievable as it sounds, the slices won't melt or lose their shape. Another trick is to fold tiny cubes of jellied sauce into meat-loaf mixture, or muffin or coffee-cake batter.

Heat any of the cranberry beverages. Sipped hot, they're bracing warmers on a shivery day.

Freeze jellied cranberry sauce for a wonderfully easy and refreshing relish for meat. Here's how: Place the unopened can in the freezer for several hours, then open, push out the frozen block and slice.

Make sauce by *baking* fresh cranberries rather than simmering them. Follow your favorite recipe for the amounts of berries, sugar and water needed, combine in a baking dish and cover tightly, then bake about an hour in a moderate oven (350°).

Cranberry Floating Island
Makes 8 servings

    1 cup cranberries, washed and stemmed
 1¼ cups sugar
  ½ cup water
    4 eggs
  ¼ teaspoon cream of tartar
  ¼ teaspoon salt
    3 cups milk
    1 tablespoon finely chopped candied orange
      peel
 1½ teaspoons orange extract

1 Combine cranberries with ¼ cup of the sugar and water in a small saucepan. Heat to boiling, then cook, stirring several times, 5 minutes, or until thickened. Press through a sieve into a small bowl. (There should be ½ cup.) Set aside for Step 2. (Set remaining sugar aside for Steps 3 and 6).
2 Separate eggs, placing whites in a large bowl and yolks in the top of a medium-size double boiler for Step 6.
3 Add cream of tartar and salt to egg whites; beat until foamy-white and double in volume. Sprinkle in ⅔ cup of the remaining sugar, 1 tablespoon at a time, beating all the time until sugar dissolves completely and meringue stands in firm peaks. (Beating will take about 15 minutes in all with an electric beater.) Fold in cranberry mixture until no streaks of pink remain.
4 Pour water into a large frying pan to a depth of 1½ inches. Heat to boiling; remove from heat. Shape meringue into balls with a small ice-cream scoop or a large spoon; float, not touching, on hot water; poach 10 minutes. (Reheat water to boiling after poaching each batch.)
5 Lift meringues from water with a slotted spoon; drain on a cookie sheet lined with paper toweling; chill.
6 Beat remaining ⅓ cup sugar into egg yolks in top of double boiler; stir in milk. Cook, stirring constantly, over simmering water, 10 minutes, or until custard thickens slightly and coats a metal spoon. Strain into a medium-size bowl; stir in orange peel and extract; chill.
7 When ready to serve, place meringues in a large shallow bowl; pour sauce around them. Garnish with half slices of fresh orange, if you wish.

GRAPES

Most of our grape crop comes from the Pacific and Atlantic coastal regions. California, the biggest producer, starts its bounty to market as early as June; Eastern states follow suit somewhat later. For most of us, prices will be lowest and quality highest from August through December, and that's the time to enjoy these fruits out of hand, turn them into salads or fruit cups, can or freeze them or make into jelly. Excellent specialty grapes—such as Muscadine or Scuppernong, so popular in the Southeast—are often limited to local areas. It's thrifty shopping to take advantage of these favorites when their season is on.

While color and variety are two ways to identify grapes, there's another interesting distinction between Western and Eastern types. Generally speaking, the skins of Western varieties stick tightly to the pulp, so the skins are eaten too. Skins of Eastern-grown grapes, on the other hand, slide off neatly, which is why they're called "slip-skin."

How to Buy Grapes:
In most supermarkets grapes are sold by the pound or in baskets, bags, or trays. Choose bunches that are well formed, with even, plump fruit that's firm enough to stay on the stem. (Overripe grapes fall away easily, leaving bare spots in the bunch.)

Depending on the variety, fully ripe grapes tend to be fairly soft to the touch. Unlike some fruits, such as pears, grapes do not improve in either flavor or quality once they're picked.

Another guide to ripeness is color. Dark varieties should have an all-over deep rich color with no green tinge; light varieties, a silvery pale green to amber tone. As a general rule, grapes do not keep well, so buy only what you can use within two or three days.

How to Store Grapes:
Handle grapes lightly and as little as possible. Remove the store wrapper, if there is one, check the grapes and discard any soft ones. To wash or not to wash before storing seems to remain a question with strong opinion on both sides. Some say it's better to place the grapes in a colander, rinse with a gentle spray of water and dry well, spread the bunches out on a tray so the air can circulate around them and then place in the refrigerator. The opposition claims moisture speeds spoilage, so you should chill grapes first, then wash them before eating.

THE POPULAR GRAPE VARIETIES

Thompson Seedless—By far the most popular—and probably most familiar—of all, these small yellow-green oval grapes grow in large clusters, have few seeds, if any, and a sweet flavor. Besides their high rating for table use, these grapes are used for well over half of our raisin supply. Some are also commercially canned, either by themselves or in combination with other fruits, as in fruit cocktail. Season runs from June through December.

Concord—Best known as the East's blue-ribbon entry for jelly- or juice-making, but there's no sweeter treat for eating out of hand. Berries are

1070

round and bluish black with a light bloom that wipes off easily. Keep an eye out for them from late August through November.

White Muscat—Greenish yellow to white in color, these oval delicacies are used mostly for wine-making, though a few are sold on the consumer market. Learn to distinguish them from Ladyfinger grapes, which are long, loose bunches of large, pale green, very elongated fruit. Ladyfingers stay with us only through September and October; Muscats come in October.

Ribler—If you've never tried these large, round, almost black beauties, you have a treat coming. Use them to add a dramatic touch to a dessert tray or fruit centerpiece, or take advantage of their sweetness for salads and appetizers. Watch for them from August through January.

Tokay or Flame Tokay—Supply is at its peak

in autumn, although the season extends through late December. Interesting fact about Tokays: Almost all are grown within six miles of Lodi, California. You'll recognize these choice fruits by their red color, oval shape and thin skin. To seed them, or any of the varieties containing seeds, split the grape lengthwise slightly off center. Usually all of the seeds will be in the larger part and can be flicked out easily with a knife.

Emperor—Large, red and oval, with a resemblance to Tokays, these come from California in October and are a favorite holiday buy. You may still see some as late as April. The reason: They keep well in storage, which has enabled modern marketing experts to stretch their season considerably.

Malaga—From July through October, take your pick of both white and red Malagas. White are

Fruits gone high fashion: Banana Split Pie (bottom), Paradise Bavarian (top) and Molded Grape Compote. They're showy desserts but a snap to prepare.

medium-size bunches of medium-size round grapes, whereas the red fruit is slightly larger.

Niagara—Yellow-green and large with a thin skin, this is a popular Eastern table grape available from September to November.

Cardinal—A cross between Tokay and Ribier, Cardinals vary in color from red to black. Fruit is round and large and, when fully mature, tastes very much like a Muscat. Season begins in mid-June.

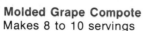

Molded Grape Compote
Makes 8 to 10 servings

    3 envelopes unflavored gelatin
1¼ cups sugar
5½ cups water
    1 cup lemon juice
    3 large seedless oranges, peeled and sectioned (1½ cups)
    1 cup seedless green grapes, halved and seeded
    1 large seedless grapefruit, peeled and sectioned (1 cup)
¼ cup flaked coconut

1 Mix gelatin and sugar in a small saucepan; stir in 3½ cups of the water. Heat slowly, stirring constantly, until gelatin dissolves; stir into remaining 2 cups water and lemon juice in a medium-size bowl. Chill while preparing fruits.
2 Measure 2¼ cups of the gelatin mixture into a second medium-size bowl. Place bowl in a pan of ice and water to speed setting; chill until as thick as unbeaten egg white. Fold in orange sections; spoon into an 8-cup serving bowl. Chill in refrigerator.
3 Repeat Step 2, chilling half of the remaining gelatin mixture at a time and folding grapes into one half and grapefruit into the other. Spoon grape mixture over orange layer and grapefruit mixture on top. Chill until firm.
4 Just before serving, spoon coconut in a mound in center of dessert; garnish with a small cluster of green grapes, if you wish.

Triple Fruit Flan
Bake at 375° for 15 minutes. Makes 8 to 10 servings

    1 package piecrust mix
    1 egg, beaten
    2 tablespoons sugar (for pastry)

For Triple Fruit Flan, rows of sliced peaches, whole plums and grapes line up across piecrust-mix pastry.

1 package (8 ounces) cream cheese
¼ cup sugar (for filling)
1 teaspoon grated lemon peel
2 tablespoons lemon juice
8 fresh plums, halved and pitted
3 cups sliced fresh peaches
1½ cups seedless green grapes (about 1 pound)
½ cup strawberry jelly

1 To make the flan pastry: Fold a 30-inch length of 18-inch-wide heavy-duty aluminum foil in half lengthwise, then in half crosswise, to make a rectangle, 15x9.
2 Blend piecrust mix, egg and the 2 tablespoons sugar until mixture leaves side of bowl clean.
3 Pat pastry onto foil rectangle to cover evenly. Turn up edges of foil with pastry to make a 1-inch rim on all sides, squaring off corners and pressing the extra pastry into corners to make a smooth edge. Prick well with fork. Freeze flan crust 2 hours.
4 Bake in moderate oven (375°) 15 minutes, or until golden. Cool completely in foil pan, then remove from foil to serving plate.
5 Blend cream cheese and the ¼ cup sugar until smooth in a small bowl; stir in lemon peel and juice. Spread mixture in bottom of pastry.
6 Arrange fruits in a pretty pattern over cheese layer. Melt jelly in a small saucepan. Brush over fruits. Chill till serving.

Poached Pears make a fitting finish for a robust meal.

PEARS

TIPS ON BUYING PEARS:

Five Popular Varieties:
Anjou—The principal winter pear, medium to large with a short fat neck, yellowish-green russeted skin, creamy-white flesh and spicy-sweet flavor.

Bartlett—A big long chartreuse-to-yellow pear with sweet, white, meltingly tender flesh. A dessert favorite, also the favorite for commercial canning.

Bosc—The perfect pear-shaped pear with a long tapering neck. The skin is deep yellow with cinnamon overtones, the flesh yellowish, buttery, juicy and fragrant. An excellent dessert pear.

Comice—Another dessert favorite. Comice pears are medium to large, greenish-yellow, often with a rose or russet blush. Their flesh is fine and smooth, extra juicy and sweet.

Seckel—A small, thick-skinned American pear, brownish-yellow outside, juicy and sweet inside.

While Shopping, Look for Pears that Are:
Firm-ripe or ripe but not hard.
Blemish- and bruise-free.
Of good color and aroma.

TIPS ON STORING PEARS:

Store firm-ripe or unripe pears in a humid place at room temperature (60° to 70°). They'll ripen nicely.
Store ripe pears in the refrigerator.

1073

Poached Pears
Makes 4 servings

4 firm ripe pears
½ cup blended maple syrup
¼ cup water
1 teaspoon lemon juice
2 tablespoons butter or margarine

1 Pare pears and place in large frying pan.
2 Combine syrup, water and lemon juice in 1-cup measure; pour over pears; add butter or margarine; cover.
3 Heat to boiling; simmer, basting once or twice with syrup in pan, about 40 minutes, or just until pears are tender. Cool.
4 Spoon into dessert dishes; top each with a spoonful of syrup. Serve warm.

Honey Pear Salad
Makes 6 servings

3 large pears, pared, cored, and diced
1½ cups chopped celery
¼ cup seedless raisins
3 tablespoons vegetable oil
2 tablespoons honey
2 tablespoons lemon juice
¼ teaspoon salt

1 Combine pears, celery, and raisins in a medium-size bowl.
2 Blend remaining ingredients in a cup; drizzle over pear mixture; toss to mix well.

Ginger Pears
Makes 4 servings

4 small firm ripe pears
4 tablespoons (½ stick) butter or margarine
¼ cup sugar
1 tablespoon chopped crystallized ginger
3 tablespoons water
2 tablespoons lemon juice
Light cream or table cream

1 Pare pears; quarter, core and slice thin.
2 Melt butter or margarine in a medium-size frying pan; stir in sugar, ginger, water and lemon juice; heat to boiling. Add pear slices; toss to coat with syrup mixture; cover.
3 Cook 5 minutes, or until pears are tender. Spoon into dessert dishes; serve warm with cream.

Paradise Bavarian
Makes 8 servings

⅓ cup sugar (for Bavarian)
1 envelope unflavored gelatin

⅛ teaspoon salt
4 egg yolks, well beaten
1½ cups milk
1 cup cream for whipping
1½ teaspoons vanilla
4 large firm ripe pears
1½ cups orange juice
¾ cup sugar (for pears)
Water
2 tablespoons cornstarch
¼ cup Curaçao

1 Mix the ⅓ cup sugar, gelatin and salt in a medium-size saucepan; stir in egg yolks and milk. Heat slowly, stirring constantly, just until gelatin dissolves and mixture starts to bubble. (Do not boil.) Pour into a medium-size bowl.
2 Place bowl in a pan of ice and water to speed setting. Chill, stirring several times, just until as thick as unbeaten egg white.
3 While gelatin mixture chills, beat cream with vanilla until stiff in a medium-size bowl. Fold into thickened gelatin mixture; spoon into a 4-cup mold. Chill several hours, or until firm.
4 Pare pears, halve and core.
5 Combine orange juice, the ¾ cup sugar and ½ cup water in a large frying pan; heat, stirring constantly, to boiling; simmer 2 minutes. Add pears; heat to boiling again, then simmer, turning carefully several times, 15 minutes, or until tender but still firm enough to hold their shape. Lift from syrup with a slotted spoon and place in a shallow dish; chill.
6 Measure syrup and add water, if needed, to make 2 cups. Return to pan; reheat to boiling.
7 Blend cornstarch with ½ cup water until smooth in a cup; stir into boiling syrup. Cook, stirring constantly, until sauce thickens and boils 3 minutes. Pour into a bowl; stir in Curaçao; chill.
8 When ready to serve, loosen dessert around edge with a knife; dip mold *very quickly* in and out of hot water; invert into a shallow serving bowl; Stand pears around dessert in bowl; spoon part of the orange sauce over pears. Garnish dessert with whipped cream and chopped pistachio nuts, if you wish. Serve with remaining sauce.

1074

Eve's Apple, it's said, was actually a pear. Perhaps. But these poached pears, blushing underneath their ladling of rosy melba sauce, hardly look "forbidden." Pears do have a long and illustrious history. Homer, the Greek poet, called them "a gift of the Gods." Romans carried them all over Europe and by Pliny's time some 41 different varieties were cultivated. Today there are literally thousands of varieties.

Pumpkins are for more than just pies. They make absolutely glorious soups (try the Pumpkin Bisque recipe) and puddings. They can also be prepared in much the same way as winter squash.

PUMPKINS

Pumpkins, America's golden gift to good eating, are harvested *early* in the autumn, James Whitcomb Riley's poem, ''When the frost is on the pumpkin,'' to the contrary notwithstanding. Pumpkins must, in fact, be harvested *before* ''first frost.'' They begin coming to market in August and remain available until after Thanksgiving (what would Thanksgiving be without pumpkin pie?) and Christmas.

TIPS ON BUYING PUMPKINS:

Regardless of size (and pumpkins vary tremendously in size), choose pumpkins that seem heavy for their size. Their rinds should be hard, uniformly bright orange, bruise- and blemish-free. Reject any pumpkin with soft or brown spots.

TIPS ON USING PUMPKINS:

Pies, of course, are the great American favorites, but pumpkin is also superb made into soups and puddings as the following recipes demonstrate.

●

Pumpkin Bisque
Makes 6 servings

2 tablespoons grated onion
2 tablespoons butter or margarine
1½ cups water
¼ cup instant mashed potato (from a package)
1 teaspoon salt
¼ teaspoon pepper
¼ teaspoon mace
1 tall can (14½ ounces) evaporated milk
1 cup canned or puréed pumpkin

1 Sauté onion lightly in butter or margarine in

large saucepan; add water and heat to boiling; remove from heat.

2 Beat in instant mashed potato, salt, pepper and mace until creamy-thick, then beat in evaporated milk and pumpkin. (If you have an electric blender, use it to beat mixture, a little at a time, for extra-creamy smoothness.)

3 Cover; simmer, stirring often, 15 minutes to blend flavors. Ladle into heated soup bowls or mugs.

●

Pinwheel Pumpkin Pie

Bake at 425° for 15 minutes, then at 350° for 35 minutes. Makes one 9-inch pie

½ package piecrust mix
2 eggs
1 can (1 pound) pumpkin
½ cup granulated sugar
½ cup firmly packed brown sugar
1½ teaspoons pumpkin-pie spice
1 teaspoon salt
1 tall can (14½ ounces) evaporated milk
1 can (1 pound, 13 ounces) sliced cling peaches
1 jar (12 ounces) peach preserves

1 Prepare piecrust mix, following label directions, or make pastry from your favorite single-crust recipe. Roll out to a 12-inch round on a lightly floured pastry cloth or board; fit into a 9-inch pie plate. Trim overhang to ½ inch; turn under, flush with rim; flute to make a stand-up edge.

2 Beat eggs slightly in a large bowl; stir in pumpkin, granulated and brown sugars, pumpkin-pie spice, salt and evaporated milk. Pour into prepared pastry shell.

3 Bake in hot oven (425°) 15 minutes. Lower oven temperature to moderate (350°); continue baking 35 minutes, or until custard is almost set but still soft in center. (Do not overbake; custard will set as it cools.) Cool pie completely on a wire rack.

4 Drain syrup from peach slices; pat fruit dry with paper toweling.

5 Heat preserves until hot in a small saucepan; press through a sieve into a small bowl. Holding each peach slice on a fork, dip into preserves, then arrange in a ring around edge on pie. Chill until serving time.

●

Pumpkin-Nut Pudding

Makes 12 servings

1½ cups sifted all-purpose flour
1 envelope instant mashed-potato powder (½ cup)

1¼ teaspoons baking soda
1 teaspoon salt
1½ teaspoons pumpkin-pie spice
4 tablespoons (½ stick) butter or margarine
¾ cup firmly packed brown sugar
3 eggs, separated
1 teaspoon vanilla
1 teaspoon grated orange peel
1 cup canned pumpkin (from an about-1-pound can)
¾ cup orange juice
½ cup (4-ounce jar) chopped mixed candied fruits
½ cup chopped walnuts
SPARKLY ORANGE SAUCE (recipe follows)
Walnut halves

1 Measure flour, mashed-potato powder (not flakes), baking soda, salt and pumpkin-pie spice into sifter.

2 Cream butter or margarine and brown sugar until fluffy in large bowl; beat in egg yolks, vanilla and orange peel.

3 Combine pumpkin and orange juice in 2-cup measure. Beat egg whites until they form soft peaks in medium-size bowl.

4 Sift dry ingredients, adding alternately with pumpkin mixture, into creamed butter mixture; beat well after each addition. Fold in candied fruits and chopped walnuts, then egg whites.

5 Pour into well-greased 8-cup mold; cover with foil or transparent wrap or double thickness of wax paper; fasten with string to hold tightly.

6 Place on rack or trivet in kettle or steamer; pour in boiling water to half the depth of pudding in mold; cover tightly.

7 Steam 3 hours, or until a long thin metal skewer inserted in the center comes out clean, and top springs back when lightly pressed with fingertip. (Keep water boiling gently during entire cooking time, adding more boiling water, if needed.)

8 Cool mold 5 minutes; loosen pudding around edge with knife; unmold onto serving plate. Spoon about ½ cup SPARKLY ORANGE SAUCE over; crown with walnut halves. Cut in wedges; serve with additional SPARKLY ORANGE SAUCE.

SPARKLY ORANGE SAUCE—Mix 1 cup sugar, 2 tablespoons cornstarch, 1 tablespoon grated orange peel and ⅛ teaspoon salt in small saucepan. Stir in 1½ cups boiling water gradually. Cook, stirring constantly, until mixture thickens and boils 3 minutes. Remove from heat; stir in 4 tablespoons (½ stick) butter or margarine, ½ cup orange juice and 2 tablespoons lemon juice. Serve warm. Makes 2½ cups.

1077

YEAR-ROUND TROPICAL FAVORITES

Fruit	Shopping Tips
AVOCADOS	*If avocados are to be eaten immediately,* choose fully ripe fruits, those that yield to gentle pressure of the fingers. *If avocados are to be eaten within a few days,* look for those that do not feel soft; let them ripen at room temperature. Reject any avocados with dark sunken spots, also those with cracked or broken skin. Depending on variety, an avocado's skin may be leathery and dark or smooth and bright green. The most popular size is about ½ pound.
BANANAS	Select firm bananas of good bright yellow color; avoid any that are brusied, soft, blackening or moldy. Bananas have the best flavor when their skins are bright golden and flecked with brown. Those with greenish tips (the stage of maturity at which most bananas are sold) should be allowed to stand at room temperature several days until they ripen fully.
CITRUS FRUITS (ORANGES, GRAPEFRUITS, LEMONS, LIMES, TANGERINES, KUMQUATS)	A full discussion of citrus fruits is included in the pages that follow.
PINEAPPLES	Like bananas, pineapples are harvested "green" and must be allowed to ripen several days at room temperature. Look for pineapples of good aroma with plump glossy "eyes." Avoid any that are shriveled, bruised or molding.

AVOCADOS

Chefette Fruit Plates
Ham and cheese strips plus a perky stuffed egg top a base of avocado, tomato, and papaya slices.
Makes 6 servings

1 head iceberg lettuce, shredded fine
3 medium-size avocados, halved lengthwise, peeled, seeded and sliced
3 medium-size tomatoes, cut in wedges
2 medium-size papayas, cut in 6 one-inch-thick rings, then pared and seeded
½ pound sliced cooked ham, cut in thin strips
1 package (8 ounces) sliced Cheddar cheese, cut in thin strips
STUFFED SALAD EGGS (recipe follows)
PINEAPPLE DRESSING (recipe follows)

1 Mound lettuce, dividing evenly, onto six individual serving plates; alternate avocado and tomato slices in a ring around edge.
2 Top with a papaya slice, then strips of ham and cheese. Garnish with a STUFFED SALAD EGG. Serve with PINEAPPLE DRESSING.

STUFFED SALAD EGGS—Hard-cook 3 eggs; shell, then halve lengthwise. Scoop out yolks and mash in a small bowl. Blend in 1 tablespoon mayonnaise or salad dressing, ½ teaspoon prepared mustard and salt and pepper to taste. Pile back into whites. Garnish with parsley. Chill until serving time. Makes 6 servings.

PINEAPPLE DRESSING—Blend ½ cup bottled coleslaw dressing, ¼ cup drained crushed pineapple (from an 8-ounce can) and 2 tablespoons lemon juice in a small bowl; chill. Makes about ¾ cup.

Sunburst Salad
Makes 8 servings

1 quarter wedge watermelon
1 small head romaine, washed, dried and separated into leaves
1 small cantaloupe
1 large firm ripe avocado
    LEMON DRESSING (recipe follows)

1 Cut enough balls from watermelon with a melon-ball cutter or ¼ teaspoon of a measuring-spoon set to make 2 cups. (Set any remaining watermelon aside to dice and add to fruit cup for another day.)
2 Line a large round serving plate with some of the romaine leaves; break remaining into bite-size pieces and place in center.
3 Halve cantaloupe; scoop out seeds; cut cantaloupe into 8 wedges and pare. Halve avocado, pit, peel and cut into 8 wedges. Arrange cantaloupe and avocado wedges, alternately, in a ring around edge of plate; pile watermelon balls

in center. Serve with LEMON DRESSING to drizzle over.

LEMON DRESSING—Combine ¼ cup olive oil or vegetable oil, 3 tablespoons lemon juice, 1 tablespoon honey and a dash of salt in a small jar with a tight-fitting cover; shake well to mix. Chill until serving time. Makes ½ cup.

Orange-Avocado Salad Bowl
Makes 6 servings

1 head Boston or leaf lettuce
2 oranges, pared and sectioned
1 avocado, peeled, halved and diced
    Bottled oil-and-vinegar salad dressing

1 Cut core out of lettuce; separate, wash and dry leaves. Break large ones into bite-size pieces; leave small ones whole; place in a salad bowl.
2 Arrange a ring of orange sections on top; fill center with diced avocado.
3 Just before serving, toss with enough salad dressing to coat greens well.

Jade Appetizer Cups
Grapefruit and avocado accent the flavor of lime gelatin. Frozen fruit speeds setting.
Makes 6 servings

Chefette Fruit Plate teams an unlikely combination of fruits: avocado, tomato (yes, they're fruit), papaya.

FRUITS AROUND THE CALENDAR

1 package (3 ounces) lime-flavor gelatin
1 cup hot water
1 can (about 14 ounces) frozen grapefruit sections, slightly thawed
2 tablespoons lime juice
1 small avocado, peeled, pitted and chopped
 Romaine
 Bottled Italian-style dressing

1 Dissolve gelatin in hot water in 4-cup measure. Stir in frozen grapefruit until sections separate easily; stir in lime juice. (Mixture will thicken quickly.) Fold in avocado.
2 Spoon mixture into six 5-ounce molds or custard cups; chill 3 to 4 hours, or until firm.
3 Unmold on serving plates lined with romaine.

BANANAS

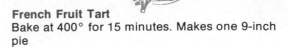

French Fruit Tart
Bake at 400° for 15 minutes. Makes one 9-inch pie

1 package piecrust mix
2 tablespoons sugar
1 egg
1 cup cream for whipping
1 package (3¾ ounces) vanilla-flavor pudding mix
1 cup milk
¼ teaspoon almond extract
½ teaspoon vanilla

What a pretty way to decorate a custard pie. Dip thin banana slices in orange juice and arrange petal-style.

1 can (about 14 ounces) frozen pineapple chunks, thawed
1 can (about 11 ounces) mandarin-orange segments
1 tablespoon conrstarch
1 banana, sliced

1 Combine piecrust mix, 1 tablespoon sugar, egg and 1 tablespoon of the cream in medium-size bowl. (Save remaining sugar for filling in Step 5, cream for Steps 4 and 5.) Mix pastry with pastry blender or fork until well blended.
2 Press into a 9-inch pie plate, making a flat rim. (Shell will be thick.) Chill at least 1 hour. Prick well all over with a fork.
3 Bake in hot oven (400°) 15 minutes, or until golden. Cool completely on wire rack.
4 Combine pudding mix, milk and ½ cup of the cream in small saucepan. Cook, following label directions; stir in almond extract. Pour into small bowl; cover with wax paper, foil or transparent wrap; chill.
5 Beat remaining cream with saved 1 tablespoon sugar and vanilla until stiff in medium-size bowl. Beat chilled pudding until creamy-smooth; fold into whipped cream. Pour into cooled pastry shell; chill while preparing fruits and glaze.
6 Drain and measure syrups from pineapple and mandarin-orange segments to make ¾ cup. Stir a little into cornstarch until smooth in small saucepan, then add remaining. Cook, stirring constantly, until mixture thickens and boils 3 minutes. Let cool slightly while arranging fruits.
7 Arrange pineapple chunks, orange segments and banana slices in 6 even-size wedge-shape sections on top of filling. (To make sure wedges will be same size, first mark guidelines on filling with tip of knife.) Spoon warm glaze over. Chill at least 2 hours. To serve, cut between fruit sections, then halve each to make 12 wedges in all.

●

Fruit Crown Cheesecake
You'll want to serve this creamy double-tier beauty—large enough for a party—right at the table.
Makes 10 servings

Fruit Mixture
2 envelopes unflavored gelatin
½ cup water
1 can (8 ounces) fruit cocktail
1 tablespoon sugar
1 tablespoon lemon juice
1 teaspoon rum flavoring or extract
Cheese Mixture
2 eggs, separated
½ cup milk

For a sunny winter dessert, try French Fruit Tart.

½ cup sugar
1 teaspoon salt
2 cups (1 pound) cream-style cottage cheese
1 teaspoon grated lemon peel
2 tablespoons lemon juice
1 teaspoon vanilla
1 cup cream for whipping
Topping
1 banana

1 Make fruit mixture: Soften gelatin in water in top of double boiler; heat, stirring constantly, over boiling water until gelatin dissolves; remove from heat.
2 Combine fruit cocktail and syrup, sugar, lemon juice and rum flavoring or extract in small bowl; stir in 1 tablespoon of the dissolved gelatin. Pour into an 8-cup mold. Let stand at room temperature until cheese mixture is made.
3 Make cheese mixture: Stir egg yolks, milk, sugar and salt into remaining dissolved gelatin in top of double boiler. Heat, stirring constantly, over simmering water, 10 minutes, or until mixture thickens slightly; cool.
4 Press cottage cheese through sieve into large bowl. (Or beat with electric mixer until creamy-smooth.) Stir in lemon peel, lemon juice, vanilla and cooled gelatin mixture.
5 Chill fruit layer in mold until sticky-firm; chill

1081

cheese mixture, stirring several times, until as thick as unbeaten egg white.

6 Beat egg whites until they stand in firm peaks in medium-size bowl. Beat cream until stiff in small bowl.

7 Fold beaten egg whites, then whipped cream into cheese mixture; pour over sticky-firm fruit layer in mold; chill until firm.

8 When ready to serve, loosen mold around edge with a thin-blade knife, then dip *very quickly* in and out of a pan of hot water. Invert onto serving plate; lift off mold.

9 Peel and slice banana; arrange slices, overlapping, in a ring around top; place a cluster of sugared grapes in center, if you wish. (To make: Dip a small bunch of green grapes into a mixture of 1 egg white beaten slightly with ½ teaspoon water in small bowl, then into granulated sugar, turning to coat grapes well. Let dry on paper toweling.)

Banana Split Pie
Bake shell at 425° for 12 minutes. Makes one 9-inch pie

½ package piecrust mix
1 pint vanilla ice cream
4 firm ripe bananas
½ cup fudge sundae sauce

2 pints strawberry ice cream
½ cup cream for whipping
½ cup strawberry sundae sauce

1 Prepare piecrust mix, following label directions, or make pastry from your favorite single-crust recipe. Roll out to a 12-inch round on a lightly floured pastry cloth or board; fit into a 9-inch pie plate. Trim overhang to ½ inch; turn under, flush with rim; flute to make a stand-up edge. Prick shell well all over with a fork.

2 Bake in hot oven (425°) 12 minutes, or until golden. Cool completely in pie plate on a wire rack.

3 About an hour before serving, chill pie shell thoroughly in freezer, then spoon in vanilla ice cream to make an even layer. Peel 2 of the bananas; halve each lengthwise and crosswise. Arrange, spoke fashion, over ice cream in shell; spoon fudge sauce over top. Return to freezer.

4 Scoop 8 small balls from part of the strawberry ice cream; place in a shallow pan; freeze firm. Spoon remaining strawberry ice cream into shell; return to freezer.

5 Just before serving, beat cream until stiff in a small bowl. Peel remaining 2 bananas; halve lengthwise and crosswise; arrange over strawberry ice cream. Top with ice-cream balls; spoon strawberry sauce, thin whipped cream into center. Cut into wedges.

This triple decker dessert doesn't look like cheesecake but it is—creamy-rich Fruit Crown Cheesecake.

Banana-Nut Loaf
This fragrantly moist bread keeps beautifully; for neat slicing, make it a day ahead.
Bake at 350° for 1 hour. Makes one 9x5x3 loaf

½ cup vegetable shortening
1 cup sugar
2 eggs
2 cups sifted all-purpose flour
1 teaspoon baking soda
¼ teaspoon salt
3 large ripe bananas, mashed (about 1 cup)
½ cup chopped walnuts
1 teaspoon vanilla

1 Cream shortening and sugar until fluffy in medium-size bowl or electric mixer; add eggs, 1 at a time, beating well after each addition.
2 Sift flour, soda and salt onto wax paper; stir quickly into creamed mixture just until blended; stir in mashed bananas, walnuts and vanilla; pour into greased loaf pan, 9x5x3.
3 Bake in moderate oven (350°) 1 hour, or until center is firm; cool 5 minutes; turn out onto wire rack; cool completely; wrap in wax paper, transparent wrap or foil; let stand 24 hours.

Bananas Brasilia
Makes 5 servings

4 tablespoons (½ stick) butter or margarine
⅓ cup sugar
3 tablespoons lemon juice
5 medium-size firm ripe bananas, peeled
4 tablespoons canned flaked coconut

1 Melt butter or margarine in a chafing dish or medium-size frying pan. Stir in sugar and lemon juice; heat, stirring constantly, until sugar dissolves.
2 Place bananas, 1 at a time, in syrup mixture, turning to coat all over.
3 Cook slowly, turning once, 10 minutes, or until bananas are heated through. Sprinkle with coconut. Serve hot, spooning any syrup in dish over bananas.

CITRUS FRUITS

SHOPPING TIPS:

At the Produce Counter:

Buy by Variety—Year round you'll find some kinds of fresh oranges, grapefruits, lemons and limes available, but like all fresh fruits, varieties change with the season, and buying what's "in" usually means lowest in price. Although all kinds are equally good sources of the vitamin C we need every day, it pays to know what's best for juicing, eating out of hand, sectioning or slicing. The photo guide that follows will help you identify the leaders.

Buy by weight and quantity—Always choose firm heavy fruits with a waxy skin. Ways of selling—by weight, number, dozen and price—differ across the country, but weight is your best guide, for the heaviest fruit—not the biggest—is your greatest value. Oranges and grapefruits often come in handy family-size bags with special price tags, and here is a key to savings, especially if you plan to use the fruits for juice. Quantity buying pays off in another way too, as all citrus fruits keep well. Just store them in the refrigerator, or in a cool, dry, airy spot in the kitchen.

In the frozen-food cabinet:

Way out front in popularity are frozen orange, grapefruit and tangerine **concentrates** with lemonade and limeade running close behind. If yours is a juice-loving family or you have a home freezer, it pays to stock up. If you have only the freezer compartment of your refrigerator for storage, buy for a week at a time, and choose the can size that can be used up within a day.

On the grocery shelves:

Here you'll find small and jumbo cans of sweetened or unsweetened, single or blended fruit juices, plus orange or grapefruit sections, or a mixture of the two.

In the Dairy Case:

Fruits and juices are relative newcomers to the dairy case, but all offer a wealth of convenience. Orange and grapefruit juices—in cartons or bottles—are ready to drink, and sectioned fruits in glass jars are handy for breakfast, salads or fruit cups. At home, keep all of these products chilled.

CITRUS FRUITS IDENTIFIED

Winter's sun shines brightest in the growing areas—Florida, California, Texas and Arizona—that supply us with citrus fruits all year long. Although most of us can't identify every kind that's available, it pays to learn a few salient characteristics of the most popular varieties. Here's a handy guide for your quick reference:

1083

FRUITS AROUND THE CALENDAR

Navel Orange—Seedless, with a deep orange, thick pebbly rind, and a favorite for eating out of hand. In season from October through May.
Valencia Orange—Ideal for juice. Medium to large, golden orange color, smooth thin rind, few seeds. Peak season: February through November.
Hamlin Orange—Medium-size, thin smooth rind, almost seedless, and excellent for juice. Biggest supply available from October to February.
Parson Brown Orange—Medium-size, pebbly rind, yellow-orange, some seeds, and wonderfully juicy. Available October through February.
Temple Orange—Deep reddish, thin pebbly rind, peels and sections easily, tastes somewhat like a tangerine. At its best from November to April.
Lime, Lemon—Persian lime (only kind in our markets) has dark green thin rind, pale green meat, sour flavor. Lemon needs no introduction.
Tangerine—Small to medium, deep orange. This zipper-skin fruit peels and sections easily, has a tangy flavor. Look for it November to February.
Marsh Grapefruit—Popular, small to medium, smooth thin yellow rind, pink or white meat, nearly seedless. Season extends from October to June.
Duncan Grapefruit—Large, pale yellow, thin rind, some seeds, lots of juice and superior flavor. Its season runs October through May.
Kumquat, Calamondin—Used mostly in gift boxes. Kumquats are orange, oval, bitter. Calamondin, tiny and orange, tastes very sour.

ABOUT GRATED CITRUS PEEL

1 lemon = about 1½ teaspoons grated peel
1 lime = about 1 teaspoon grated peel
1 orange = about 1 tablespoon grated peel
Tip: Grate peel before cutting fruit, and work with a light touch, removing *only* the colored part of the peel, not the bitter white pith underneath.

ABOUT CITRUS JUICE

1 lemon = about 2 tablespoons juice
1 lime = 1 to 2 tablespoons juice
1 orange = ⅓ to ½ cup juice
Note: All quantities given are for medium-size fruits.

●

Fruits Royale
Makes 6 servings

2 large seedless oranges
1 large seedless grapefruit
1 large ripe pear

1 large ripe banana
¼ cup sugar

1 Pare a thin layer of peel from 1 orange with a vegetable parer, then cut into slivers. Place in a small saucepan; add water to cover; simmer 15 minutes; drain.
2 While peel cooks, pare white membrane from cut orange and skin and membrane from whole orange and grapefruit; section all three fruits, working over a medium-size bowl to catch juices; add sections to juice. Pare, quarter, core and slice pear; peel banana and slice; add both to other fruits.
3 Stir sugar into drained orange peel; heat slowly, stirring constantly, just until sugar dissolves. Fold hot mixture into fruits, making sure banana slices are covered; chill.
4 Spoon into serving dishes; garnish each with a walnut half, if you wish.

●

Golden Fruits Ambrosia
Strips of mellow candied fruit peels give this sparkling dessert a company air.
Makes 6 to 8 servings

3 seedless oranges
2 seedless grapefruits
1 can (about 14 ounces) frozen pineapple chunks, thawed
2 tablespoons lemon juice
1 package (10 ounces) frozen sliced peaches, thawed

1 Peel and section oranges and grapefruits into separate small bowls. (Save all orange peels and peel from 1 grapefruit to make FRUIT-PEEL SPARKLES [*recipe follows*], if you wish.)
2 Drain syrup from pineapple into 1-cup measure; stir in lemon juice.
3 Arrange 2 mounds each of orange and grapefruit sections, and pineapple chunks in a shallow glass serving dish. Pour pineapple-juice mixture over.
4 Arrange sliced peaches in a ring on top; pour any peach juice over fruits. Top with several strips of FRUIT-PEEL SPARKLES, or crystallized ginger, if you wish.

●

Orange-Lemon Cream
Makes 6 servings

1 envelope unflavored gelatin
1 cup orange juice
2 eggs, separated
½ cup sugar
3 tablespoons lemon juice

Fruits Royale, served in a tall wine goblet, are elegant enough for any party. Because this is a light dessert, precede with a rich and filling entré.

1085

Golden Fruits Ambrosia, unlike the dish Greek Gods doted upon, has both pineapple and peaches added.

1 teaspoon grated lemon peel
1 cup cream for whipping

1 Soften gelatin in ¼ cup of the orange juice in a small saucepan; heat slowly, stirring constantly, just until gelatin dissolves. Remove from heat.

2 Beat egg yolks with ¼ cup of the sugar until fluffy in a medium-size bowl. (Remaining ¼ cup sugar is for meringue in Step 3.) Stir in the dissolved gelatin mixture, then the remaining ¾ cup orange juice, lemon juice and peel. Chill, stirring often, 50 minutes, or until as thick as unbeaten egg white.

3 While gelatin mixture chills, beat egg whites until foamy-white and double in volume in a medium-size bowl; beat in remaining ¼ cup sugar, 1 tablespoon at a time, until meringue stands in firm peaks. Beat ½ cup of the cream until stiff in a small bowl. (Remaining cream is for garnish in Step 6.)

4 Fold cream, then meringue into thickened gelatin mixture until no streaks of white remain; spoon into a 5-cup mold. Chill several hours, or until firm.

5 To unmold, run a sharp-tip, thin-blade knife around top of mold, then dip mold *very quickly* in and out of a pan of hot water. Cover mold with serving plate; turn upside down; carefully lift off mold.

6 Beat remaining ½ cup cream until stiff in a small bowl; spoon on top; garnish with mandarin-orange segments, if you wish.

●

Fruit-Peel Sparkles
Ginger gives this confection a subtle spicy flavor. Gelatin in the coating keeps it soft and moist. Serve, too, as candy.
Makes 1½ pounds

    Peel from 3 seedless oranges
    Peel from 1 grapefruit
2½ cups sugar
  1 tablespoon light corn syrup
  1 teaspoon ground ginger
  ⅛ teaspoon salt
1½ cups water
  1 teaspoon unflavored gelatin (from 1 envelope)

1 Cut orange and grapefruit peels into ⅛-inch-thick strips with scissors.

2 Place in large saucepan with water to cover. Heat to boiling; simmer 15 minutes; drain. Re-

Orange Crown Jewels are a luscious baked confection.

peat cooking with fresh water, then draining, two more times. Return peels to saucepan.

3 Stir in 2 cups sugar, corn syrup, ginger, salt and 1 cup water. (Save remaining ½ cup sugar for Step 6 and ½ cup water for Step 5.)

4 Heat slowly, stirring often, to boiling, then simmer, stirring often from bottom of pan, 40 minutes, or until most of syrup is absorbed; remove from heat. (Do not overcook, as syrup will caramelize and turn brown.)

5 Soften gelatin in saved ½ cup water in 1-cup measure; stir into hot peel mixture, stirring until gelatin dissolves. Let stand until cold.

6 Lift out strips, 1 at a time; roll in saved ½ cup sugar in pie plate to coat well. Place in single layer on wax paper-lined tray or cookie sheet to set.

7 Store in a container with tight-fitting cover. This peel keeps fragrant and moist for weeks.

Orange Crown Jewels

Bake at 300° for 25 minutes. Makes 8 stuffed oranges

> 8 large seedless oranges
> 3 cups water
> 3 cups granulated sugar
> ½ cup vegetable shortening
> ½ cup firmly packed brown sugar
> 2 eggs
> 1 cup sifted all-purpose flour
> 1 teaspoon pumpkin-pie spice
> ½ teaspoon salt
> 1½ cups golden raisins
> ½ cup chopped candied pineapple
> ½ cup chopped candied red cherries
> ½ cup toasted slivered almonds (from a 5-ounce can)

1 Cut a thin slice from the stem end of each orange; cut out pulp, being careful not to puncture peel. (Set pulp aside to press through a sieve for a breakfast beverage or to add to fruit punch.)

2 Place orange cups and top pieces in a kettle; cover with cold water. Heat to boiling; cover. Simmer 10 minutes; drain. Repeat cooking and draining two more times, using fresh water each time. (If any bits of pulp remain in shells, scoop out with a teaspoon.)

3 Heat the 3 cups water with granulated sugar, stirring constantly, in same kettle just until sugar dissolves; add orange cups and tops. Simmer, uncovered, stirring several times with a wooden spoon, until syrup registers 220° on a candy thermometer. (Syrup will fall slowly off a spoon in two drops that run together.) Remove from heat at once; let stand overnight.

4 The next morning, reheat mixture slowly, then cook, turning oranges often and basting with syrup, 5 minutes. Lift cups and tops carefully from syrup; turn cups upside down on wire racks to drain while mixing cake batter. Pour any remaining syrup into a cup and set aside for Step 7.

5 Cream shortening in medium-size bowl with a spoon or electric mixer; add brown sugar gradually, beating until fluffy. Beat in eggs, 1 at a time, until fluffy. Stir in flour, pumpkin-pie spice and salt just until blended; fold in fruits and almonds. Spoon into orange cups to fill about ¾ full; set top pieces in place. (Spoon any remaining batter into a greased custard cup; cover with foil, and steam, then bake along with filled oranges.)

6 Place a rack in a kettle or small roasting pan; pour in water to within ¼ inch of top of rack. (It should not touch oranges.) Place filled oranges on rack; cover. Steam, adding more water, if needed, 45 minutes. Remove oranges and place in a large shallow baking pan.

7 Bake in slow oven (300°) 25 minutes. Remove oranges and brush with the saved syrup; roll in coarse sugar in a pie plate to coat well, if you wish. (This sugar is sold in specialty shops.) Cool oranges completely on wire racks.

8 Wrap each orange in transparent wrap and store in the refrigerator at least two or three days to mellow. (They will remain fresh in refrigerator for as long as two weeks.) Decorate tops with sprigs of Christmas greens, if you wish. To serve, cut into wedges.

Tangerine Salad Bowl

Makes 6 servings

> 3 medium-size tangerines, peeled and sectioned
> 1 small onion, peeled, sliced, and separated into rings
> ¼ cup bottled thin French dressing
> 2 tablespoons honey
> 6 cups broken mixed salad greens
> 3 pitted ripe olives, slivered

1 Place tangerine sections and onion in separate small bowls. Drizzle each with French dressing and honey; toss lightly to mix. Chill.

2 When ready to serve, place greens in a large salad bowl. Arrange tangerine sections in a rosette on top; place onion rings around edge; pile olive slivers in center. Drizzle with any remaining dressing in bowls.

1087

FRUITS AROUND THE CALENDAR

Tangerine Sunshine Mold
Makes 8 servings

    2 envelopes unflavored gelatin
    ¼ cup sugar
    ¾ teaspoon salt
    2 cups water
    1 can (6 ounces) frozen concentrated tan-
       gerine juice
    3 tablespoons lemon juice
    1 can (about 1 pound, 5 ounces) pineapple
       tidbits, drained
    ½ cup grated pared raw carrot

1 Soften gelatin with sugar and salt in one cup of the water in a medium-size saucepan; heat, stirring constantly, until gelatin dissolves; remove from heat.
2 Stir in remaining water, concentrated tangerine and lemon juices. Chill until as thick as unbeaten egg white.
3 Fold in pineapple and carrot; spoon into a 6-cup mold. Chill several hours, or until firm.
4 Unmold onto a serving plate; serve with your favorite mayonnaise or salad dressing, if you wish.

Snowball Citrus Cup
Makes 8 servings

    2 grapefruits, pared and sectioned
    4 oranges, pared and sectioned
    1 can (about 14 ounces) frozen pineapple
       chunks
      Seeds from half a pomegranate
    1 pint lemon sherbet

1 Combine grapefruit and orange sections and juice with pineapple chunks and a few pomegranate seeds in a medium-size bowl; cover; chill.
2 When ready to serve, spoon fruits into eight sherbet glasses; top each with a small scoop of sherbet; garnish with a few more pomegranate seeds.

1088

Spiced Grapefruit Compote
Makes 6 to 8 servings

    1 package (12 ounces) mixed dried fruits
    1 jar (about 2 ounces) tiny cinnamon candies
    ¼ teaspoon grated lemon peel
    1½ cups water
    ¼ cup quick-cooking tapioca
    ¾ cup sugar
    1 can (1 pint, 2 ounces) unsweetened grape-
       fruit juice
    3 grapefruits

The secret of Snowball Citrus Cup—pomegranate seeds.

1 Combine dried fruits, cinnamon candies, lemon peel and water in a medium-size saucepan. Heat to boiling; simmer 25 minutes, or until fruits are tender. Pour into a large bowl.
2 Combine tapioca, sugar and grapefruit juice in same saucepan; let stand 5 minutes. Heat slowly, stirring several times, just until mixture comes to a full rolling boil; pour over cinnamon-fruit mixture.
3 Pare grapefruits; section over a medium-size bowl to catch the juice; remove seeds, if any. Fold fruit and juice into dried-fruit mixture.
4 Spoon into individual serving dishes; serve warm.

Minted Grapefruit Cup
Makes 6 servings

1 jar (10 ounces) mint jelly
¼ cup sugar
4 grapefruits

1 Heat jelly with sugar until melted in a small saucepan; cool slightly.
2 Pare grapefruits; section over a medium-size bowl to catch the juice; remove seeds, if any.
3 Pour mint syrup over fruit. Chill at least an hour to blend flavors. Serve cold.

Grapefruit Ambrosia
Makes 6 servings

3 grapefruits
1 large orange
3 tablespoons sugar
Flaked coconut

1 Pare grapefruits; section over a medium-size bowl to catch the juice; remove seeds, if any.
2 Pare orange; slice thin crosswise. Overlap slices around edge in a shallow bowl; mound grapefruit in center.
3 Drizzle juice over fruits; sprinkle with sugar, then coconut. Chill.

Lemon Cream Royale
Makes 10 servings

2 envelopes unflavored gelatin
1 cup sugar
6 eggs, separated
1¼ cups water
1 tablespoon grated lemon peel
½ cup lemon juice
1½ cups cream for whipping

1 Prepare a 4-cup soufflé or straight-side bak-ing dish this way: Cut two strips of wax paper 12 inches wide and long enough to go around dish with a 1-inch overlap; fold in half length-wise. Wrap around dish to make a 2-inch stand-up collar; hold in place with cellophane tape or a rubber band and a paper clip.
2 Mix gelatin and ¾ cup of the sugar in a medium-size saucepan; beat in egg yolks until fluffy-light, then water.
3 Cook slowly, stirring constantly, until gelatin dissolves completely and mixture thickens; remove from heat. Pour into a large bowl; stir in lemon peel and juice.
4 Place bowl in a pan of ice and water to speed setting. Chill, stirring often, just until as thick as unbeaten egg white.
5 While gelatin mixture chills, beat egg whites until foamy-white in a medium-size bowl. Beat in remaining ¼ cup sugar, 1 tablespoon at a time, until meringue forms soft peaks. Beat cream until stiff in a medium-size bowl.
6 Fold whipped cream, then meringue into thickened lemon mixture. Spoon into prepared dish.
7 Chill several hours, or until firm. Serve plain, or garnish with more whipped cream, sprigs of mint, and a lemon rose, if you wish. (To make a lemon rose: Choose a medium-size lemon, and, starting at the blossom end, pare off peel in one continuous long strip. Wind strip round and round to form a rose pattern.)

Lemon Dream Pie
Bake shell at 275° for 1 hour. Makes one 9-inch pie

4 eggs, separated
¼ teaspoon cream of tartar
½ teaspoon salt
½ teaspoon vanilla
2 cups sugar
4 tablespoons cornstarch
1½ cups water

½ cup lemon juice
2 tablespoons butter or margarine
1 cup cream for whipping

1 Generously butter a 9-inch pie plate.
2 Beat egg whites with cream of tartar, ¼ teaspoon of the salt, and vanilla until foamy-white and double in volume in a large bowl. Beat in 1 cup of the sugar, 1 tablespoon at a time, beating all the time until sugar dissolves completely and meringue stands in firm peaks. (Beating will take about 25 minutes in all with an electric beater.)
3 Spoon meringue into pie plate. Spread almost to side of plate, hollowing center and building up edge slightly to form a shell.
4 Bake in very slow oven (275°) 1 hour, or until firm and lightly golden. Cool completely in pie plate on a wire rack.
5 While shell bakes, mix remaining 1 cup sugar, cornstarch and ¼ teaspoon salt in a medium-size saucepan. Stir in water, then beat in egg yolks and lemon juice.
6 Cook, stirring constantly, until mixture thickens and boils 3 minutes; remove from heat. Stir in butter or margarine until melted; pour into a medium-size bowl; cover. Chill until completely cold.
7 Beat cream until stiff in a medium-size bowl. Layer lemon filling, alternately with whipped cream, into meringue shell. Chill about 12 hours before cutting. (To match design on pictured pie, layer about three fourths of the lemon filling and cream into shell. Attach a plain tip to a pastry bag; spoon remaining lemon filling into bag; press out in rings on top of pie. Repeat with whipped cream, filling in spaces between lemon rings.)

●

Sugared Lemon Crown
Bake at 350° for 50 minutes. Makes one 9-inch cake

2¼ cups sifted cake flour
1 teaspoon baking powder
½ teaspoon salt
¾ cup (1½ sticks) butter or margarine
1½ cups granulated sugar
3 eggs
1 tablespoon grated lemon peel
2 tablespoons lemon juice
⅔ cup milk
10X (confectioners' powdered) sugar

1 Butter an 8-cup tube mold; dust lightly with flour, gently tapping out any excess.
2 Sift flour, baking powder and salt onto wax paper.
3 Combine butter or margarine, granulated

sugar and eggs in large bowl of electric mixer; beat at high speed 3 minutes. (Do not underbeat.) Slowly beat in lemon peel and lemon juice.
4 Add flour mixture, a third at a time, alternately with milk, beating at low speed just until blended. Scrape bowl often between additions. Pour into prepared pan.
5 Bake in moderate oven (350°) 50 minutes, or until top springs back when lightly pressed with fingertip.
6 Cool cake in mold on a wire rack 10 minutes. Loosen around edge with a knife; invert onto rack; cool completely. Before serving, sprinkle lightly with 10X sugar.

●

Lemon Blossom Tart
Bake shell at 400° for 20 minutes. Makes 8 servings

1 package piecrust mix
2 tablespoons sugar (for pastry)
4 eggs
½ cup sugar (for filling)
2 teaspoons grated lemon peel
¼ cup lemon juice
4 tablespoons (½ stick) butter or margarine
1 cup cream for whipping

1 Combine piecrust mix, the 2 tablespoons sugar and 1 of the eggs in a medium-size bowl. Mix with a fork until well blended.
2 Press evenly over bottom and up side of a 9-inch round layer-cake pan, making rim even with edge of pan. (Shell will be thick.) Prick well all over with a fork.
3 Bake in hot oven (400°) 20 minutes, or until golden. Cool completely in pan on a wire rack.
4 Beat remaining 3 eggs slightly in the top of a double boiler; stir in the ½ cup sugar, lemon peel and juice and butter or margarine. Cook, stirring constantly, over hot (not boiling) water 10 minutes, or until very thick. Pour into a medium-size bowl; chill until completely cold.
5 Beat cream until stiff in a medium-size bowl; fold into lemon custard.
6 Remove pastry shell carefully from pan; place on a large serving plate; spoon lemon filling into shell. Garnish with a pinwheel of candied lemon slices, if you wish. Chill 1 to 2 hours before serving.

Three luscious desserts for lemon lovers: (left) Lemon Blossom Tart, pound-cake-like Sugared Lemon Crown (behind) and meringue-crusted Lemon Dream Pie (at right).

Heavenly Lemon Soufflé can be served in its baking dish instead of being inverted; garnish with a lemon slice.

Heavenly Lemon Soufflé

Bake at 350° for 30 to 40 minutes. Makes 6 to 8 servings

5 eggs
  Butter or margarine
6 tablespoons sugar
¼ teaspoon salt
2 teaspoons grated lemon peel
3 tablespoons lemon juice

1 Separate eggs, putting whites into large bowl, yolks into small bowl.
2 Coat a 6-cup mold with softened butter or margarine; dust evenly with about 1½ tablespoons sugar (save rest of sugar for Step 4).
3 Beat egg whites with salt just until stiff enough to hold their shape but still moist. (Overbeating will make them dry.)
4 Beat egg yolks until thick, gradually adding remaining 4½ tablespoons sugar; beat in grated lemon peel and lemon juice.

5 Fold egg-yolk mixture very lightly into beaten egg whites until no streaks of the yolk or white appear; pour into prepared mold; set in baking pan on oven rack; fill pan with boiling water to depth of 1 inch.
6 Bake in moderate oven (350°) 30 to 40 minutes, or until puffy-light and firm in center.
7 Loosen soufflé around edges with knife; shake and tip gently to loosen at sides; place heated serving plate over soufflé; invert; lift off mold (buttery syrup coating mold will flow over soufflé); serve at once, plain or with whipped cream.

Lime Angel Pie

Makes one 9-inch pie

1 cup sugar
1 envelope unflavored gelatin
¼ teaspoon salt
½ teaspoon vanilla

1092

4 eggs, separated
½ cup water
¼ cup lime juice
2 teaspoons grated lime peel
  Green food coloring
1 baked 9-inch pastry shell
1 cup cream for whipping
2 tablespoons 10X (confectioners' powdered)
  sugar

1 Combine ½ cup of the sugar, gelatin, salt and vanilla in top of a double boiler.
2 Beat egg yolks slightly in a small bowl; stir in water and lime juice; stir into gelatin mixture.
3 Cook, stirring constantly, over simmering water, 10 minutes, or until gelatin dissolves and mixture coats a metal spoon. Strain into a small bowl; stir in lime peel and a drop or two of food coloring to tint green. Chill, stirring several times, until as thick as unbeaten egg white.
4 Beat egg whites until foamy-white and double in volume in a large bowl; sprinkle in remaining ½ cup sugar, a tablespoon at a time, beating all the time until meringue stands in firm peaks.
5 Place bowl of meringue in a pan partly filled with ice and water. Fold thickened gelatin mixture into meringue until mixture mounds on a spoon. Spoon into pastry shell; chill 3 to 4 hours, or until firm.
6 Just before serving, beat cream and 10X sugar until stiff in a medium-size bowl; spoon over filling. Sprinkle with grated lime peel, if you wish.

Almond-Lime Loaf
Bake at 350° for 1 hour and 10 minutes. Makes 1 loaf, 9x5x3

3 cups sifted all-purpose flour
1 cup sugar (for batter)
3 teaspoons baking powder
1 teaspoon salt
¼ teaspoon baking soda
1 package (3 ounces) sliced unblanched almonds
2 tablespoons grated lime peel
1 egg
1 cup milk
5 tablespoons butter or margarine, melted
3 tablespoons lime juice
2 tablespoons sugar (for topping)

1 Grease a loaf pan, 9x5x3.
2 Sift flour, the 1 cup sugar, baking powder, salt and soda into a large bowl; stir in ¾ cup of the almonds and 1 tablespoon of the lime peel.
3 Beat egg well with milk in a small bowl; stir in 4 tablespoons of the melted butter or margarine and 2 tablespoons of the lime juice. Add all at once to flour mixture; stir just until evenly moist. Spoon into prepared pan; spread top even.
4 Combine remaining almonds and 1 tablespoon melted butter or margarine with the 2 tablespoons sugar in a cup; spoon evenly over batter.
5 Bake in moderate oven (350°) 1 hour and 10 minutes, or until a wooden pick inserted in center comes out clean. Cool in pan on a wire rack 10 minutes. Loosen around edges with a knife; turn out onto rack; place right side up.
6 Drizzle remaining 1 tablespoon lime juice over loaf, then sprinkle remaining 1 tablespoon lime peel on top. Cool completely.
7 Wrap loaf in wax paper, foil or transparent wrap. Store overnight to mellow flavors and make slicing easier. Cut in thin slices.

PINEAPPLE

FRESH PINEAPPLE CUTUPS
PLAIN AND FANCY

Fix Slices or Wedges This Way:

1 Twist off spiny crown of pineapple; slice fruit ¾ inch thick. Now remove rough skin by cutting close to inside rim to keep from wasting fruit.
2 Speed the job of taking out eyes and any brown or soft spots with the tip of a grapefruit knife. Curved end works fast, cutting just deep enough.
3 Core slices with a knife or small round of doughnut cutter. Whole rings look showy for fruit-salad plates; dainty wedges are nice for desserts.

Fix "Boats" This Way:

1 Cut a fragrantly ripe pineapple in quarters lengthwise, right through its leafy crown. Slide a knife under core to loosen, cutting not quite to ends.
2 Remove fruit in one piece by cutting close to round shell base. Here, too, a grapefruit knife and a sawing motion will free it with little effort.
3 Halve fruit crosswise, then quarter each piece to make eight even wedges. Slide each, alternately backward and forward, under the core.

1093

Pineapple makes a tasty casserole dish. To see for yourself, try Polynesian Chicken in Fresh Pineapple Shells.

A FRUITY SERVING BOWL

Fresh pineapple makes a handy dish in which to serve chicken, especially a Polynesian sweet-and-sour chicken like this one made famous by Curt Yocom's Restaurant in Iowa City, Iowa.

Polynesian Chicken in Fresh Pineapple Shells
Bake at 350° for 1 hour and 5 minutes. Makes 4 servings

1 broiler-fryer, weighing about 3 pounds, cut up
¼ cup vegetable oil
2 tablespoons soy sauce
2 tablespoons Worcestershire sauce
1 tablespoon monosodium glutamate
1 teaspoon garlic powder
1 teaspoon salt
1 teaspoon cracked black pepper
1 teaspoon leaf rosemary, crumbled
2 firm ripe pineapples
1 can (about 1 pound, 14 ounces) fruits for salad
4 teaspoons cornstarch
½ cup sauterne wine
¼ cup flaked coconut

1 Place chicken pieces, bone side up, in a greased baking pan.
2 Combine vegetable oil, soy sauce, Worcestershire sauce, monosodium glutamate, garlic powder, salt, pepper and rosemary in a cup; brush part over chicken.
3 Bake in moderate oven (350°) 25 minutes. Turn chicken pieces; brush with remaining oil mixture. Continue baking 40 minutes, or until chicken is tender and golden.
4 While chicken bakes, halve pineapples lengthwise, cutting through leafy crown. Cut all around fruit to loosen from shells; lift out; cut out cores. Cut fruit in large chunks; set fruit and shells aside.
5 Drain liquid from canned fruits and stir into cornstarch in a medium-size saucepan; stir in wine. Cook, stirring constantly, until sauce thickens and boils 3 minutes; fold in fruits and pineapple. Heat just until hot.
6 Arrange chicken pieces in pineapple shells; place on serving plates. Spoon hot fruit sauce over chicken; sprinkle with coconut.
Note—If fresh pineapple is not available, substitute 1 can (1 pound, 4 ounces) pineapple chunks in pure juice. Drain well before adding to sauce.

Pineapple Crown Salad
Makes 8 servings

1 large pineapple
2 cups (1 pint) strawberries
2 medium-size seedless oranges
1 small firm ripe avocado
½ cup dairy sour cream
½ cup mayonnaise or salad dressing
¼ cup 10X (confectioners' powdered) sugar

1 Cut a slice, ¾ inch thick, from crown and bottom of pineapple; stand pineapple upright. Holding a sharp, long-blade knife vertically, insert into pineapple about ½ inch in from rind, then cut all around fruit to loosen from shell; push out fruit. Quarter lengthwise; slice core from each piece; cut fruit into bite-size pieces. Place in a large bowl.
2 Wash strawberries; hull and halve. Pare one of the oranges and section. Peel avocado; halve, pit and slice. Toss all with pineapple. Chill.
3 Grate 1 teaspoon peel from remaining orange, then squeeze 2 tablespoons juice; blend both with sour cream, mayonnaise or salad dressing, and 10X sugar in a small bowl.
4 Stand pineapple shell on a large serving plate; spoon fruit mixture into shell. Serve dressing separately.

Pineapple-Shrimp Boats
Quarters of fresh fruit and a cutting trick make pretty servers for seasoned shrimps.
Makes 4 servings

1 bag (1½ pounds) frozen deveined shelled raw shrimps
½ cup vegetable oil
¼ cup lemon juice
1 teaspoon sugar
½ teaspoon paprika
½ teaspoon ground ginger
½ teaspoon salt
1 large ripe pineapple
½ cup mayonnaise or salad dressing
1 tablespoon catsup

1 Cook shrimps, following label directions; drain. Place in a medium-size bowl.
2 Combine vegetable oil, lemon juice, sugar, paprika, ginger and salt in a jar with tight-fitting lid; shake well to mix. Pour over shrimps; cover. Chill at least an hour to season and blend flavors.
3 Quarter pineapple lengthwise, cutting through leafy crown. Loosen fruit from rind and

1095

FRUITS AROUND THE CALENDAR

core with a sharp knife, but do not cut core at ends; leave both fruit and core in place. Slice fruit crosswise into serving-size pieces; chill if fixed ahead.

4 When ready to serve, drain shrimps, saving marinade in a cup. Place pineapple quarters on serving plates; push cut pieces of fruit alternately to back and front; fill the spaces with shrimps.

5 Blend ¼ cup of the saved marinade with mayonnaise or salad dressing and catsup in a cup. Spoon into four tiny serving cups or salt dishes; set each on a plate in a lettuce cup, and garnish pineapple with a twist of lemon, if you wish.

Upside-Down Pineapple Cake
Bake at 350° for 1 hour. Makes 8 servings

Topping

- 4 tablespoons (½ stick) butter or margarine
- ¾ cup firmly packed light brown sugar
- ⅛ teaspoon salt
- 1 can (about 1 pound, 4 ounces) pineapple spears, drained
- 12 maraschino cherries, quartered

Cake

- 2 eggs, separated
- 2 cups sifted cake flour
- 2½ teaspoons baking powder
- ½ teaspoon ground ginger
- ¼ teaspoon salt
- ½ cup (1 stick) butter or margarine
- 1 cup granulated sugar
- ½ teaspoon grated lemon peel
- ½ teaspoon vanilla
- ½ cup milk
- ½ cup finely chopped walnuts

1 Make topping: Melt butter or margarine in baking pan, 9x9x2; stir in brown sugar and salt. Cook, stirring constantly, over low heat, until bubbly; remove from heat. Arrange pineapple spears and cherries in rows on sugar mixture.

2 Make cake: Beat egg whites just until they stand in firm peaks in small bowl.

3 Sift flour, baking powder, ginger and salt onto wax paper.

4 Cream butter or margarine with sugar until fluffy in large bowl with spoon or electric mixer; beat in egg yolks, lemon peel and vanilla. Blend in dry ingredients alternately with milk; fold in

For a sensational summer luncheon, try Pineapple Shrimp Boats. The fruit is fresh but the shrimp is frozen.

walnuts and beaten egg whites. Pour over fruits in pan.

5 Bake in moderate oven (350°) 1 hour, or until top springs back when lightly pressed with fingertip.

6 Cool on wire rack 5 minutes; cover pan with serving plate; quickly turn upside down, then carefully lift off baking pan. Serve warm or cold, topped with plain or whipped cream or vanilla ice cream.

TWO TROPICAL EXOTICS: MANGOES AND PAPAYAS

HOW TO EAT A MANGO:

Somewhat round in shape, mangoes vary in size from a plum to an apple, with a smooth thin skin and a yellow to reddish-yellow color, depending on the variety. When ripe, the meat is juicy, soft and aromatic, with a flavor similar to pineapple and apricot combined.

Although some mangoes are used green for preserves, chutney or pickles, ripe ones are usually enjoyed raw. To fix them, chill well first. Then halve and seed to eat like a melon with a squeeze of lemon or lime; or pare, cut up and mix into fruit cup; or slice and turn into this summery salad:

Mango Tropicale
Makes 4 servings

GINGER-HONEY DRESSING (recipe follows)
2 ripe mangoes
1 can (about 9 ounces) sliced pineapple
2 medium-size firm ripe bananas
Leaf lettuce

1 Fix GINGER-HONEY DRESSING.
2 Pare mangoes, remove seeds and slice fruit thin.
3 Drain syrup from pineapple (save to sweeten fruit punch); quarter pineapple slices. Peel bananas and slice diagonally.
4 Line a large serving plate with lettuce; pile mango slices in center; arrange pineapple and banana slices around edge. Garnish with a slice of lime, if you wish, and serve with GINGER-HONEY DRESSING.

GINGER-HONEY DRESSING—Combine ½ teaspoon ground ginger, ½ teaspoon salt, ¼ teaspoon paprika, ½ cup vegetable oil, ¼ cup

Papaya Coupe teams this tropical exotic with berries.

lemon juice and 3 tablespoons honey in a jar with a tight-fitting lid. Shake well to mix. Makes about 1 cup.

HOW TO EAT A PAPAYA:

Papaya (or tropical "tree melon") is a big orange fruit with butter-smooth flesh; it tastes a little like peach, a little like pineapple, a little like *pine*. It's delicious chilled and sliced with a squirt of lime or lemon or halved and filled with grapes and berries. It also makes splendid pickles and preserves.

Papaya Coupe
Makes 4 servings

2 firm ripe papayas
Lettuce
1 cup blueberries
1 cup seedless green grapes, halved
1 lime, cut in 4 wedges

1 Halve papayas; scoop out seeds; place on lettuce-lined salad plates.
2 Fill hollows with blueberries and grapes. Garnish each with a whole strawberry, if you wish, and serve with lime wedges to squeeze over.

1097

A rosy paprika-dusted Onion
Aster blooms from a dinner plate.

Olive slices, pimiento slivers
and celery crescents are
quick and colorful garnishes.

GARNISHES, TRIMMINGS

AND TOPPINGS

GARNISHES, TRIMMINGS AND TOPPINGS: GADGETS FOR GARNISHES, GIVE FAMILY FOODS A PRETTY BUILDUP

Food should *look* as good to eat as it tastes. A large part of making food beautiful is teaming—in one dish or dinner—foods of contrasting but compatible colors, textures, shapes and sizes. The other part is simply adding a few judicious garnishes, not so many as to overload the platter and overwhelm the dinner, merely enough to add eye-appeal and interest.

There are dozens of ways to garnish foods—with fancily cut fruits and vegetables, with decorative toppings, with frills of greenery, ruffs of whipped cream, piped-on borders of mashed potatoes.

Most garnishes—even the showiest—are deceptively easy to make. Turn the pages and learn how.

GADGETS FOR GARNISHES

Pretty garnishes like these—easily made with gadgets that do the work virtually by themselves—are so simple to fix that you'll be tempted to decorate even your everyday meals. For almost all garnishes it's best to start with chilled foods. If you're adding a perishable garnish to hot food, bring the garnish, chilled, to the table and add it to the food there.

With radish cutter face up, push radish (with leaf end up) onto the gadget until the radish is cut to ⅔ its length. Pull the radish carefully, straight up from the cutter. Put the cut radish into ice and water so the petals will spread. Serve the "rosebuds" as a garnish with cold cuts or salad or by themselves on ice.

Orange Peeler

Cranberry Flowers

Butter Curls

You can make a long strip of orange peel by running this peel cutter all around an orange. The cutting edge lifts only the peel—no white part. The flat blade can be used either to guide the narrow cutting edge or to cut wider strips for bows or twists. The cutter, which works equally well for a left-handed person, is a real boon for cutting fresh peel for fruitcakes or candied fruits.

Dainty butter or margarine curls lend elegance to any table and are easy to fix with a butter curler. Holding the serrated edge of butter curler against the top of a very cold one-pound brick of table spread, press just enough to raise a thin strip (one that's too thick won't curl). Pull the hook gently toward you. To avoid breaking the curl, push—don't pull—it off the hook. Place the curl in ice and water. Wipe the hook with a dampened dishcloth after making each curl. Chill the finished curls until used. Take them to the table in a dish of crushed ice or on a dish set into ice.

"Flowers" cut from jellied cranberry sauce add color to a sliced-chicken sandwich. Little jelly or aspic cutters for this garnish come in 12 different shapes in a metal box. Cut jelly into slices as thick as the molds. Press the cutter into the slice as close to the outside edge as possible. Lift the cutter and the cut jelly, using a small spatula or knife with a wide blade. Placing the jelly over the food it will garnish, gently push the jelly out of the cutter. The cutters can also be used to cut slices of vegetables to garnish a salad or to make canapés.

1100

GIVE FAMILY FOODS A PRETTY BUILDUP

Once in a while it's fun to take just a few extra minutes to add a bright garnish or trim to everyday dishes—and how your family will appreciate the surprise! Simple ideas shown here for pie, cake, salad, and meat play up the holiday season and make showy conversation pieces for your table.

Thanksgiving Special—Gay autumn leaves atop pumpkin pie salute the harvest season and double as a flavor dividend. Cut leaves from process-cheese slices, then lightly mark veins with a cotton-tipped stick dipped in diluted red food coloring.

Thanksgiving Special

Star-Bright

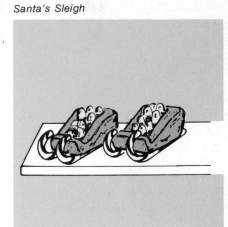
Santa's Sleigh

Salad Bouquet

Star-Bright—Simple artistry with gold-and-white candy corn on a two-layer cake catches the spirit of the holidays yet takes so little effort. Another time, use the same idea on frosted cupcakes as a treat or favor for a children's party.

Salad Bouquet—Striped radishes nestled in frilly lettuce leaves circle a shimmery mold. To fix radishes, make about six cuts lengthwise into each, then cut a thin strip behind each line, slanting knife in slightly, and lift out strip.

Santa's Sleigh—Little folks will be delighted with these miniature servers for candy. Bake your favorite cake mix in toy loaf pans. (One package makes eight cakes.) "Carve" each to resemble a sleigh; frost; set on candy-cane runners.

Yule Jewel—A candy tree, simple enough for young cooks to make, sprouts atop a frosted flat cake. Use stick candy for the trunk, canes of whatever size you wish for branches, a peppermint round for top and pillow-shape mints for base.

Blossoming Beauty—Decorate glazed ham with sunny pineapple tidbits placed, petal style, around a jellied cranberry-sauce cutout. Add trim after meat comes from oven so cranberry sauce doesn't melt; glaze will hold garnish in place.

1101

Yule Jewel

Blossoming Beauty

GARNISHES, TRIMMINGS AND TOPPINGS

HOW TO MAKE VEGETABLE FLOWERS

Onion Aster: Peel a large onion and trim off ends; to fashion petals, make 16 evenly spaced cuts around onion from outside edge almost to center, cutting down to within ¼ inch of bottom. Chill onion in ice water until petals spread and curl slightly. Drain on paper toweling, brush with vegetable oil and sprinkle with paprika.

Beef Blossoms: Pare a medium-size fresh beet and cut off stem and root ends. Make 3 to 4 horizontal cuts around top edge of beet, then, holding knife at an angle, make a second cut just above each line and lift out narrow strip of beet. Continue making rows of cuts around beet, about ½ inch apart, until you reach the bottom. Wrap and chill until ready to use.

Radish Roses: Choose bright red medium-size radishes. Scrub well and cut off root end. To form petals, make 4 to 5 cuts down sides of radishes, about ¼ inch in from edge and to within ⅛ inch of bottom. Then, if you wish, halve each petal vertically with a sharp knive to form a double row of petals. Chill in ice water until petals open.

Carrot Chrysanthemum: Wash and scrape 2 long carrots; shave each into paper-thin strips with a vegetable parer. Trim each strip to an about-5-inch length, rounding ends slightly. (Job goes fast if you stack several strips and use kitchen scissors for cutting.) Thread 10 or 12 strips through middle onto a wooden pick; spread ends, spoke fashion. Chill in a bowl of ice and water several hours, or until strips curl, petal style. To make radish center, trim root and leafy top from 1 large radish. Holding radish, root end up, make deep cuts lengthwise with very sharp knife, then turn radish and cut again at right angle to first cuts. Chill until petals open slightly. Stick onto wooden pick in center of carrot flower.

MORE PRETTY VEGETABLE AND FRUIT GARNISHES

Olive Dumbbell and Bundle
So simple! Just place a pitted ripe olive on each end of a thick carrot stick, or thread several sticks through the olive.

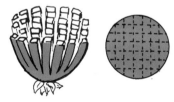

Radish Pompon
Slice a trimmed radish one way, then crosswise, almost through to stem. Chill in ice water until opened into a puffy flowerlike ball.

1102

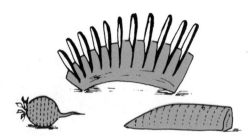

Cucumber Accordion
Cut 3-inch lenghts of split pared cucumber; slice thin almost to flat side. Poke thin radish slices in cuts.

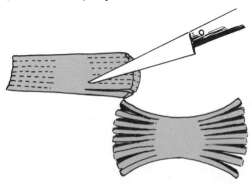

Celery Flute
Slit 2-inch lengths of celery into narrow strips, cutting from ends toward middle. Chill until strips curl slightly.

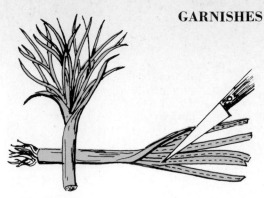

Lemon Cartwheel
Perfect for fish dishes. And how easy to fix. Cut small notches all around the rim of lemon slices with a knife or scissors.

Onion Ruffle
Trim root from a green onion, then shred the top down about three inches. Place in a bowl of ice and water to curl. Nice touch for a salad-relish plate.

Carrot Curl
Shave scraped carrot into paper-thin slices; wrap around finger, then hold with a wooden pick. Chill in ice water until crisp.

Pickle Fan
Slice small pickles into 5 or 6 strips, starting at tip end and cutting almost to stem. Spread slices to form open fans.

EYE-CATCHING WAYS TO TRIM A CASSEROLE

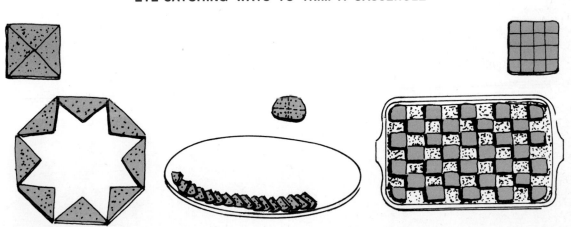

1103

Make these perky toppers with sliced bread
Quarter slices, diagonally and place, points in, around edge of a casserole to form a pretty star design. Or cut bread in cubes and arrange, checkerboard fashion, on top. Even party rye, quartered and lined up around a baking dish, looks as special as its name.

Go gay with cheese
Many casserole recipes call for cheese toppings, and here it's the arrangement that counts. Use a whole slice and several triangles to make the whirling star; strips make the chevron.

Make a jaunty kebab
For an eye-catching extra for fruit cup or salad, mold cream cheese into balls of varying sizes, roll in chopped walnuts, and thread onto a kebab stick. Pretty, too, for a fruit-gelatin dessert.

Turn hard-cooked eggs into flower fancies
Fun to "grow," they add a bright note to a casserole after baking. To fix these, overlap slices around an olive; or cut wedges for petals and arrange with parsley between. For the dainty cup, make saw-tooth cuts around middle of egg; separate halves. Sieve yolk, mix with mayonnaise, and pile back in whites.

Fix sunny curls
To make these curlicues, shave thin strips from a small block of process Cheddar with a vegetable parer or knife. Roll them around your finger; slide off gently and chill. Pile onto an apple pie.

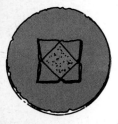

Try these twists on pastry
For an extra-dressy look, twist strips of pastry into ropes, or cut a cross in a pastry round and turn points back so the filling peeks through. Want to be really artistic? Cut flower and leaf shapes with truffle cutters; use poppy seeds or herbs for centers.

Shape snowy petals
Beat a bit of sugar and spice into cream cheese; measure level teaspoonfuls, and push off spoon with your thumb. Place the petals, rounded sides up, in a double ring, on a fruit pie or tart.

Dress a cold platter

Here are four simple how-to's: Roll long cheese slices lengthwise (cut in half) or square slices diagonally. Stack rounds with bologna and cut in wedges, or wrap meat around a thin stick of cheese.

Grow golden "apples"

Scoop tiny rounds from a block of cheese with a melon-ball cutter; top with whole-clove stems. Or cut flat shapes from cheese slices; dust with paprika for rosy cheeks. Serve atop apple crisp.

Pipe a perky ruffle

Cheese-and-fruit dessert takes a fancy turn here. Just press fluffy cream cheese through a pastry tube around your favorite upside-down cake. It makes a nice change from a whipped-cream topper.

SOME BERRY PRETTY WAYS TO DECORATE DRINKS AND DESSERTS

Rosette

This show-off dresses a pie or cheesecake so prettily, and you can make it any size. Slice berries lengthwise, then outline a circle in center of dessert with some of the largest slices, points out. Continue with overlapping circles to center, using smallest slices last. Finish with a whole berry.

Rosy Kebab

Just one berry can create a big effect. Thread it on a kebab stick and use for garnishing appetizer or dessert fruits.

Double-Berry Cup

Make cuts lengthwise from tip almost to stem in a large berry; spread "petals." Place whole berry, tip up, in center.

Snowdrop

Real rushed? Try this easiest of all trims. Dip berry in 10X sugar to coat generously, leaving the hull on for a handle.

Sipper Treat

For a bright touch for summer beverages, alternate plump berries with other fruits on colorful drinking straws.

HERB/SPICE

POWER

**HERB (AND SPICE) POWER:
COOKING WITH HERBS,
COOKING WITH SPICES AND
BLENDS, SEASONING
TRICKS TO BOOST YOUR
COOKING FAME, HOW
TO MAKE POTPOURRIS,
HOW TO MAKE POMANDERS**

Astonishing to think what impact a pinch of herb or spice has in a recipe. Astonishing, too, to realize that wars were fought over herbs and spices, that kingdoms were won and lost—fortunes, too.

Herbs and spices are so very available today that we tend to take them for granted. And yet, not so very many years ago, only the rich and the royal could afford them. Small wonder, for many herbs and spices grew in far and exotic lands (primarily Indonesia and Africa) and traveled thousands of miles, most of them arduous, over desert and sea before reaching the kitchens of kings. Spice merchants, in order to keep competitors away and protect their trade, spun wild tales about the lands where spices grew, stories well populated with fire-breathing monsters, venomous serpents, giant man-eating birds.

Today, the most exotic herbs and spices are only as far away as the nearest supermarket. And their cost is mere pennies. There's no reason, then, not to try them all. The herb and spice charts in the pages that follow show you how to use herbs and spices in recipes. There are also directions for making old-fashioned potpourris and pomanders, which rely heavily upon herbs and spices for their lovely scents.

WHEN YOU COOK WITH HERBS

YOUR HERB CHOICES	BASIL Fresh and spicy and a never-fail seasoner for all tomato dishes	DILLWEED Its feathery green leaves add a delightfully mild bouquet	MARJORAM Fragrantly sweet herb of the mint family—a joy to all cooks	OREGANO Mint herb, too, with a flavor that tastes a bit like thyme	ROSEMARY "For remembrance." Valued for its subtle tang	SAVORY A beginner's choice for a basic mild-flavor herb	TARRAGON Has a piquancy all its own. Use sparingly, for it's strong
When you fix: **BEEF**	Stew or goulash: Add ½ teaspoon to recipe for 4 to 6 servings		Roast: Rub onto meat or crumble a big pinch into roasting pan	Meat loaf: Stir ½ teaspoon into mixture for 2-pound loaf	Roast: Another good choice to sprinkle into roasting pan	Pot roast: Mix with flour to rub on meat before browning	Boiled beef: Making gravy? Season with a discreet dash
VEAL	Scaloppine: Crush a generous pinch and stir into tomato sauce	Cutlets in sour cream: Sprinkle into the rich so-good sauce	Roast: Mix with flour, salt, and paprika to season meat for cooking	Stew: Be miserly, for it's strong— ⅛ teaspoon for 4 servings		Braised chops: Crush a smidgen, add to pan when half cooked	Jellied loaf: Simmer a pinch in broth; strain for jellied base
PORK HAM		Spareribs: Bake with sauerkraut seasoned ever so generously	Roast and chops: Experts vote a soupçon or two about right	Braised pork shoulder: Add a big pinch to pan as meat browns	Ham patties or loaf: Crumble in a small pinch before shaping	Stuffed chops: Season 1 cup stuffing with ¼ teaspoon	
LAMB	Barbecued shanks: Add to seasoned marinade for a mellow flavor	Stew: Sprinkle over stew or stir into it while it is cooking	Potpie: Stir ⅛ teaspoon into pastry or biscuit topping	Braised riblets: Sprinkle lightly on ribs or add to basting sauce	Roast: Perfect herb for all cuts. Just sprinkle into roasting pan	Scotch broth: Stir just a bit into soup before dishing it up	
CHICKEN TURKEY DUCK	Cookout chicken: Stir 1 teaspoon into 2 cups barbecue sauce	Chicken salad: Use lightly in the salad or as a pretty garnish	Oven chicken: Mix a pinch into melted butter for coating chicken	Roast duck: Sprinkle lightly inside duck or in baking pan	Chicken stew: Add to broth during cooking; strain for gravy	Hot turkey sandwich: Stir a bit into gravy while heating	Chicken caccia-tore: Crumble a big pinch and add to sauce
FISH SEAFOOD	Seafood cocktail: Crumble a speck into tomatoey sauce-dip	Baked, broiled or poached fish: It enhances all. Use as you like	Stuffed fish: Mix into dressing or sprinkle into pan for baking	Fish chowder: Use sparingly; add just before dishing it up		Seafood salad: Toss a smidgen with salad or add to dressing	Butter, cream, tartare sauces: Perfect season-er for them all
POTATOES		Baked or boiled: Stir lightly in-to butter sauce or sour cream	Scalloped: Crush a touch and add to the seasoned flour mixture	Hash brown: Sprinkle a bit into drippings before browning		Salad: Mix with dressing; add to potatoes while still warm	German-fried: Crush and mix with other sea-sonings in pan
PEAS LIMAS GREEN BEANS	In herb butter: Heat with butter or margarine, then spoon over	In cream sauce: Stir ½ teaspoon into each 1 cup sauce	In salad dress-ing: Be miserly. Just a pinch does wonders		Simple seasoning: Add a few sprigs to cooking water in saucepan	With sour cream: Spoon the creamy topping over; add herb lightly	In sweet-sour sauce: Crush a generous pinch; add to sauce
TOMATOES	Broiled, stewed, fried: An always right, all-round seasoner	Sliced fresh: Use to taste along with salt and pepper	Scalloped: Mix with buttered bread cubes and sprinkle over	Juice appetizer: Add a bit to other seasonings and heat	Spaghetti sauce: Try just a touch for an elusive flavor	Soup: Sprinkle lightly over bouillon or cream soup	Salad bowl: Let a pinch mellow in the salad dressing

	BASIL	DILLWEED	MARJORAM	OREGANO	ROSEMARY	SAVORY	TARRAGON
BROCCOLI CABBAGE CAULIFLOWER		Simple seasoner-garnish: Add to sauce or sprinkle over vegetable	Au gratin: Put a smidgen in cheese sauce or crumb topping		With corned beef and cabbage: Add a pinch to the cooking water	In salad dressing: Allow about ¼ teaspoon for 1 cup dressing	In sweet-sour sauce: Use the same as with peas and beans
EGGS CHEESE	Welsh rabbit: Stir in just a bit for a pleasant zing	Scrambled eggs: Use amount to suit your own taste	Egg salad: Try just a pinch or two in the salad dressing	Pizza: A "must" to sprinkle on top of the cheese before baking		Cheese fondue: Stir a bit into egg-milk base before baking	Eggs Benedict: Crumble and add a dash to the sauce topper
RICE SPAGHETTI NOODLES	Spanish rice: Stir ½ teaspoon into prepared tomato sauce	Buttered noodles: Try just a sprinkle over hot noodles	Canned spaghetti in tomato sauce: Add ½ teaspoon to each can	Spaghetti with meat sauce: Let herb simmer in sauce	Minestrone: Add a very light sprinkle as the soup simmers	Noodles in sour cream: Use sparingly, tossing with cream	

WHEN YOU COOK WITH SPICES AND BLENDS

	ALLSPICE	CARDAMOM	CHILI POWDER	CURRY POWDER	GINGER	ITALIAN SEASONING	PUMPKIN-PIE SPICE
YOUR SPICE AND BLEND CHOICES	Like a blend of cloves, nutmeg, cinnamon. Comes whole or ground	Thin pods hide gingery black seeds to crush. Sold ground also	Blend of rich racy spices—the flavor spark to chili con carne	Deep gold-hued blend of exotic herbs and spices of the Far East	An aromatic, pungent root sold fresh or dried or ground	One of the newer herb blends and a good all-round seasoner	Easy alternate when you need cinnamon, cloves, nutmeg, ginger
When you make:							
BREAD ROLLS SWEET BUNS	Use sparingly in either yeast or baking-powder doughs	Flavor Old World coffeecakes, buns, and pastries with just a soupçan		Add ½ teaspoon to white bread dough for a subtle touch		Heat a bit in butter or margarine to brush on French bread	Add to flour in same amount as sum of all the other spices
SOUPS CHOWDERS			Zesty dress-up for thick bean chowder. Use dash in tomato soup	Use lightly for a teaser flavor, more for a good zippy curry bite	Borrow an Oriental seasoning tip and add a hint to chicken broth	Sprinkle a little into minestrone, garbanzo, and tomato soups	Season potato-onion chowder with a dash of this spicy mix

	ALLSPICE	CARDAMOM	CHILI POWDER	CURRY POWDER	GINGER	ITALIAN SEASONING	PUMPKIN-PIE SPICE
CASSEROLES	A pinch in beef, pork, veal or lamb dishes adds a good zip	Use sparingly with meat balls and chicken dishes. It's spicy	Many Mexican recipes call for it. It's hot—so measure carefully	Use 2 teaspoons to season a 6-serving casserole mildly hot	Add to taste in gravies for beef, pork, veal, and vegetable combos	Gives a lift to meat and fish dishes. Crush it just a bit	Making biscuit topping? Stir ¼ teaspoon into 1 cup of mix
SALADS DRESSINGS	Just a touch in meat salads—especially ham— adds spiciness	It enhances most dressings. Try sparingly on fruits, too	A sprinkling gives zing to all kinds of picnic salads	Try a dash in chicken salad or its dressing for an exotic touch	Think of it for seasoning fruit salad lightly; dressing, too	Sprinkle over any green salad for a fragrant spunky seasoner	Sprinkle buttered toast with sugar, then lightly with this mix
SANDWICHES		Add with a very light touch to ham salad and cheese mixes	Baked-bean—sandwich enthusiasts say a dash makes the difference	Stir a little into chicken- or egg-salad, and cheese fillings		Hot tip: Top bread with slices of tomato, herb, and cheese; grill	
DIPS SPREADS DUNKS	Mix a dash in deviled ham or liver pâté to spread on toast	Stir a speck into dip of minced clams and sour cream	Just the right seasoning for guacamole dip (mashed avocado)	Give sour cream or chili sauce a big dash for dunking shrimps		Make your own herb cheese with soft Cheddar. Add cautiously	
SAUCES GRAVIES	Just a bit does wonders to meat gravies such as beef, pork, veal	Add a dash to your favorite barbecue or basting sauce	Stir lightly into cocktail sauce or sauce for spaghetti	Curry-sauce tip: Cook long and lazily to bring out best flavor	Beat a little into sweetened whipped cream to top fruit	Use in spaghetti sauce; add a speck to gravy for roast pork	Stir some into lemon sauce; add, too, to sweet or sour cream
COOKIES	Try a soupçon in fruit bars and applesauce cookies. Good!	Gives an elusive "bite" to holiday butter and sugar cookies	*TIPS FOR THE HERB AND SPICE COOK*		Recipes for big soft cookies and crisp snaps call for this spice		To substitute for other spices: Measure to nearest round figure
PIES	Add a dash or two to sugar when making summer fruit pies	Making a coffee or an orange chiffon pie? Use a dash	· Cook with one herb or spice at a time until you learn its characteristics. And measure lightly, for flavor builds.		Stir ¼ teaspoon into buttery cookie or crumb piecrusts	Pizza is "pie" in Italian, and here is the herb to sprinkle over	Named for its most favored use. Try, too, in apple pie
CAKES FROSTINGS	Add a spicy dash when making holiday fruitcake or its frosting	Stir lightly into vanilla, coffee or orange butter frosting	· Add herb for stews, soups, and sauces during the last hour of cooking. · Give herb time to season in uncooked dishes like salad dressings, sauces, marinades.		Use, of course, in gingerbread. Try a whit, too, in applesauce cake		Blend it into sugar-and-water icing to drizzle over spicecake
PUDDINGS	Sprinkle a dash or two into hard sauce for Christmas plum pudding	Add a pinch to vanilla pudding mix for an enticing flavor	· Want to know how strong or mild an herb is? Crush a bit in the palm of your hand, let it warm slightly, then sniff. · Keep herb and spice containers tightly covered to save flavor.		Stir a bit into eggs and milk when making rice or bread pudding		Sprinkle ever so lightly onto cup custards before baking
PICKLES PRESERVES	Use the whole spicy berry when making pickled tiny cucumbers	Goes well with homemade fancies like watermelon-rind preserves	Gives a "hot" touch to chopped tomato relish and piccalilli	Pickled carrot and green-bean sticks like curry. Use sparingly	An all-round spice for jams, jellies, pickled and spiced fruits	Use in any recipe that calls for zesty mint-like oregano	"Spice" fresh or canned peaches, pears, apples with this blend

SEASONING TRICKS TO BOOST YOUR COOKING FAME

A saucy extra, lively topper, or a touch of herb or spice can lift an everyday dish right into the "let's have it again" class. Here are ideas—none fussy—for perking up the flavors of main dishes, vegetables, salads.

MAIN DISHES WITH A DIFFERENCE

Dilled Skillet Pork—Favorite pickles are the flavor key. Sauté pork chops, as usual, until tender. Thinly slice a dill pickle or two and arrange slices on top of each chop. Sprinkle lightly with brown sugar and dill-pickle juice. Cover; steam 10 minutes to blend flavors. Garnish with a sprig of fresh dill, if you wish.
Glazed Lamb Broil—A mix of marmalade and curry powder makes this sparkling glaze for lamb chops—shoulder, rib or loin cuts. Just season ¼ cup orange marmalade with ¼ teaspoon curry powder and brush lightly onto chops when they are about done. Continue broiling just until tops turn invitingly bubbly.
Tivoli Scrambled Eggs—The Danes have a way with nutmeg and here it's a flavor-garnish for breakfast or supper scrambled eggs; Cook the eggs as you like them, then sprinkle lightly with freshly grated nutmeg.
Savory Meat-Pie Topper—For a pleasing smoky flavor and extra richness, substitute 2 tablespoons bacon or sausage drippings for shortening when making pastry to cover meat pie.
Soy Burgers—Season ground beef with 1 teaspoon salt for each 1 pound meat, shape into patties and pan-fry. Just before turning, brush with soy sauce; turn; brush other side. Continue cooking until done as you like them.

SALAD-VEGETABLE SEASONERS— BRIGHT AS SPRING

Mimosa Salad Bowl—Hard-cook an extra egg or two at breakfast time to sieve and sprinkle over a bowl of crisp salad greens. Add a few shredded almonds for crunchiness, and toss with your favorite homemade oil-and-lemon dressing.
Lemonnaise Cream—Serve it warm over green vegetables, cold with fruit or sea-food salads. To make: Mix ¼ cup mayonnaise or salad dressing with 1 teaspoon lemon juice, ¼ teaspoon sugar and a dash of liquid red pepper seasoning or cayenne.

Salad Sprinkles—How they can vary that favorite green salad! A few to remember: Wheat germ, pine nuts, grated Parmesan cheese, snipped chives, sesame seeds.
Barbecued Baked Potatoes—Rub the skins lightly with salad oil, dust all over with chili powder and bake. Serve with dairy sour cream and crumbled canned French-fried onion rings to sprinkle over.
Creamed Celery, Onions, or Cabbage—For a delightful elusive flavor, stir ¼ teaspoon bottled aromatic bitters into each 1 cup white sauce.
Deviled Green Beans—Season buttered green beans with a discreet spoonful of prepared mustard or horseradish.

HOW TO MAKE HERB VINEGARS

A gourmet treat that's so easy to fix—and what welcome hostess gifts they make!

Tarragon Vinegar
Pack an 8-cup jar or bottle loosely with fresh tarragon; fill with 8 cups cider vinegar; cover. Let stand 4 to 5 days to season; strain. When ready to bottle, fill containers with seasoned vinegar; slide a fresh sprig of tarragon into each; seal. Makes 8 cups.

Dill Vinegar
Pack an 8-cup jar or bottle loosely with fresh dill; fill with 8 cups white vinegar; cover. Let stand 4 to 5 days to season; strain. When ready to bottle, fill containers with seasoned vinegar; slide a fresh sprig of dill into each; seal. Makes 8 cups.
Wrapping tip: Fancy jars or bottles from variety stores make handsome use-again containers. Fresh herbs tend to darken in vinegar, so bottle as near the day of use as possible.

HOW TO MAKE POTPOURRIS

"Gather ye rosebuds"—and herbs and spices—and make fragrant potpourri sachets. Blend ingredients, "age," then store in decorative jars. Remove the tops for a garden-fresh scent year round, or wrap the potpourri in ribbon-tied bits of tulle or organdy and tuck in a dresser drawer.

There are two types of potpourri: Moist and dry. The moist type is made by layering partially dried petals of fragrant roses with salt to cure. This mixture is aged and then the other ingredients are added. For dry potpourri, petals and flowers are thoroughly dried first, and then mixed with the other ingredients.

For dry potpourri, pick flowers that are freshly

1111

opened in the morning, just after the dew has dried off. Petals and flowers should be as perfect as possible; discard any that are bruised or damaged. Place flowers in thin layers on paper toweling, cheesecloth-covered screens or baking sheets, away from heat and direct sunlight in a shady place that has a good circulation of air. If possible, rest screens in such a way that air can circulate under them. Heat, and especially light, will result in a loss of fragrance and color.

Specific directions for preparing petals for MOIST ROSE POTPOURRI are included in the recipe.

When salt is listed in the ingredients, it is important to use coarse (kosher) salt, *not* iodized.

Except when otherwise noted, whole spices are preferred to the packaged, powdered spices because the scent of the freshly crushed spice is stronger. However, if any of the ones listed are only available powdered, they may be substituted, adding a teaspoonful at a time to obtain the scent you desire.

All ingredients used in these recipes should be available at your local grocery store or druggist.

Be sure to let the potpourri age in a tightly closed jar, shaking or stirring from time to time, and keeping it closed when not in use to preserve the fragrance.

Never use perfume or cologne in a potpourri. Do not use culinary (food extracts) oils found in supermarkets.

Do not be afraid to experiment with spices, herbs and flowers that are not on these lists. Keep records of your experiments. Your own special potpourri, in a pretty jar, perhaps with the recipe attached, makes a delightful gift.

●

Dry Rose Potpourri

1 quart dried rose petals
¼ to ½ cup dried rose buds (damask roses work well)
1 ounce orris powder
1 tablespoon ground mace
2 tablespoons whole cloves
1 vanilla bean (cut or broken into small pieces)
1 tablespoon whole cardamom in pods (crushed)
2 sticks cinnamon (crushed)
20 drops oil of orange,
OR: 10 drops each oil of lemon and oil of orange

Combine dried rose petals and rosebuds with orris. Lightly mix with hands or wooden fork and spoon in a large bowl. Blend mace, cloves, vanilla bean, cardamom and cinnamon separa-

1112

tely. Add to rose mix. Blend well. Drop orange (orange and lemon) oil over mix; stir gently. Place in jars with tight-fitting lids (or in double plastic bags—each bag sealed with twisters). Store unopened for six weeks, shaking often. When ready to use, place in a pretty container. Stir gently; a rich fragrance will rise.

Moist Rose Potpourri

2 quarts rose petals (fresh fragrant varieties— pick in the morning)
Coarse salt (kosher type) . . . do NOT use iodized salt
2 ounces orris powder
¼ ounce ground mace
¼ ounce ground cloves
1 small stick cinnamon (crushed)
¼ ounce ground nutmeg
¼ ounce ground allspice
5 drops oil of rose or oil of jasmine

Gather freshly opened, unbruised petals in a variety of colors. Spread out on paper toweling and let dry until they lose about half their bulk and have a leathery (half-dry) look. Place in large jars or crocks with lids, layering roses with salt. Continue alternating layers of roses and salt (ending with salt) only until container is two-thirds full. Cover tightly and store away from heat and light for three weeks. (If a liquid forms, press down petals with the back of a spoon and pour off residual liquid.) After three weeks, remove from jars. Shake away salt. If petals have caked together, flake lightly with fingers. Place petals in a large bowl. Mix orris and all spices together separately and add to roses. Return to jars with tight-fitting lids. Store *unopened* for six weeks. When ready to use, add oil gradually, stirring gently.

●

Marigold and Mint Potpourri

1 cup of dried marigold flowers
1 cup leaf thyme
1¼ cups whole peppermint leaves
¾ cup leaf basil
1 cup coarse salt

Blend herbs and salt carefully as above, being careful not to crush the herbs. Mix in marigolds. Ripen and store as in COUNTRY HERB POTPOURRI (recipe follows).

●

Country Herb Potpourri

¼ cup dried lemon peel
¼ cup dried orange peel

¼ cup dried lime peel
1 cup leaf marjoram
1½ cups leaf rosemary
½ cup leaf sage
1 or 2 bay leaves (coarsely broken)
¼ cup summer savory
1 cup coarse salt

To prepare your peels, pare fruits with a vegetable parer; try not to pick up the white pith. Spread strips of peel on a plate to dry thoroughly. Break them up coarsely; measure out desired amounts. The bright yellow, orange and green peels will add color to the potpourri, in addition to the citrus scent. Blend the herbs and peels together in a big bowl. Mix with hands or wooden spoons, and crush the herbs very slightly. Add salt and mix thoroughly. Let ''ripen'' in jars with tight-fitting lids, away from light and heat, for four to six weeks; then place in decorative jar with a tight-fitting lid. When ready to use, open jar, stir potpourri gently and leave the cover off for a while. Replace cover tightly when not in use. This will prolong the life of the fragrances. This mixture has a refreshing citrus-herbal fragrance. If you want a stronger citrus scent, you may increase the amount of peel.

●

Lavender Jar Potpourri

1 cup lavender leaves
2 cups lemon verbena leaves
1 ounce orris powder
1 cup dried carnation petals (optional)
1 cup any dried white flowers and petals

Blend flowers and leaves in a bowl with hands or wooden fork. Sprinkle on orris. Mix gently. Store in jars with tight-fitting lids for a month, away from heat and light, shaking from time to time. Then place in decorative jars; open and stir gently to use.

●

Spice Potpourri

1 tablespoon anise seed, crushed
1 teaspoon whole allspice, crushed
5 or 6 nutmegs, coarsely broken
1 teaspoon powdered ginger (optional)
4 or 5 sticks cinnamon, coarsely broken
¼ cup whole cloves
½ teaspoon ground cinnamon
2 or 3 whole vanilla beans, cut or broken into small pieces
1 cup coarse salt

Perhaps the easiest way to crush the small spices is with a mortar and pestle. The nutmegs

should be broken with a hammer on a carving board. Mix all the spices carefully together as above; add salt. Mix thoroughly. Ripen and store as in COUNTRY HERB POTPOURRI (recipe precedes). This potpourri has a wonderfully exotic scent without being heavy or overpowering and is particularly appropriate for a man's room or closet.

HOW TO MAKE POMANDERS

Pomander Apples

Apples
Whole cloves (about 1 small box for each apple)

Beginning at the top of the apple, insert cloves as closely together as possible. Cover the entire apple in this way, trying not to leave any open spaces. The fruit will be rather soft when covered but will harden in about a week. (For quicker hardening, place pomander in warm dry place, preferably in the sun.) This will make a sweet-scented gift for a friend's closet shelf or bureau drawer. To make a hanging pomander, knot a tasseled cord around the clove-studded fruit.

●

Pomander Ball

Oranges, lemons, or limes
Whole cloves
Ground cinnamon
Orris root (available at drug stores)
Net
Colored ribbon

Wash oranges, lemons or limes and wipe dry. Make holes over the entire surface, using a skewer or bobby pin to start holes if skins are difficult to pierce. (Do not make holes in a straight line; the skins are apt to crack.) Insert whole cloves in skins so that the whole surface of the fruit is covered. Mix equal parts of ground cinnamon and orris root and put a heaping teaspoon in a small bag. Shake each clove-stuck orange, lemon or lime separately in the bag to coat well with the mixture. Wrap loosely or place in a foil-covered tray or basket. Store in a dry place until fruit shrinks and hardens, usually three to four weeks. Wrap each pomander ball in a cradle of net and tie with a colored ribbon. Give pomander balls as gifts, hang them in closets, or place them in bureau drawers for their pleasing aroma and moth-repellent quality.

**HERE'S HEALTH:
ARE AMERICANS OVERFED YET
POORLY NOURISHED? THE 4 BASIC
FOODS, GOOD NUTRITION FOR GOOD
HEALTH, THE LITTLE-KNOWN VITAMIN
THAT SPARKS VITALITY, THE MIRACLE
MINERAL THAT KEEPS YOU FIT**

ARE AMERICANS OVERFED YET POORLY NOURISHED?

By Frederick J. Stare, M.D., and Patricia Nelson, M.P.H., Department of Nutrition, Harvard School of Public Health

Are Americans overfed yet poorly nourished? Yes, too many are. And the hidden hungers of the overfed are as much cause for concern as the food deficiencies of the underfed.

Do you notice sunbathers at the beach? A great number of them are overstuffed and paunchy. Being overfed can be even more dangerous than being underfed, unless one is really starved. Just as there is malnourishment among the poor, so also is there malnourishment among the well-to-do. In both cases, important foods are missing in the diet. We must realize, also, that too much rich food is just as hazardous to your good health as too little.

Just who are these people that are overfed yet poorly nourished? Any child or adult who weighs 20 pounds—or more—than his desirable weight; any child or adult who is moderately anemic because the iron-containing pigment of the blood—hemoglobin—that transports oxygen to the body tissues is lower than it should be; any adult male whose cholesterol is higher than it should be; any child or adult who lives in a community where the water is not fluoridated.

Most of us have an Uncle Art—an overfed but

1115

Fresh fruits, Group 3 of the 4 Basic Foods, are vital to good health. Citrus fruits and melons are both excellent sources of vitamin C, watercress has vitamin

undernourished friend or relative. Art is 20, 30 or even more pounds too heavy; he is in his 40s or 50s. He is too awkward to enjoy daily exercise. He watches sports on TV and enjoys calorie-rich food and beverages while he sits out his leisure hours. Uncle Art is a prime candidate for a heart attack. His diet is filled with too many calories, too much saturated fat and too much cholesterol. (Your doctor can determine, by laboratory tests of a sample of your blood, if your cholesterol level is too high, and can prescribe a suitable diet as part of the treatment.) His wife is a good cook. She likes to surprise her husband with a new dessert and knows that she can always please him with pie or cake—especially one that is rich and creamy.

What's happening inside Art's body? The food he consumes is narrowing the blood vessels with little fat deposits all along his circulatory system. Any one of those deposits could become a perfect trap for a blood clot which might prove fatal for poor Uncle Art if it is in a vessel of the heart or brain. In a heart attack, the coronary arteries are affected. With a stroke, the blood-vessel damage is in the brain. Uncle Art may live long enough after his first attack to heed the warnings of his doctor. But Art must be told that he has a deadly disease, arteriosclerosis, and that the condition will probably continue, and even accelerate, unless he takes vigorous steps to slow it down.

Unfortunately, Uncle Art is not unique. Each year, more than 500,000 heart-attack victims keep their families and their doctors concerned. Most of these people are in the prime of life and are making their greatest contributions to society. If they had limited themselves to low-saturated fat and low-cholesterol foods, they might have avoided the onslaught of heart disease. Hopefully, Americans may soon understand the relationship of the food they consume to general body health. Overfed people, like jolly old Uncle Art, are actually malnourished.

Recently Harvard's Department of Nutrition participated in what was called the National Cooperative Diet and Heart Study. Nearly 2,000 healthy American men and their families living in Boston, Baltimore, Chicago, Minneapolis and Oakland participated. Over a two-year period they consumed a great variety of food especially prepared for this study. The food was low in saturated fats and cholesterol. Egg yolks were reduced in certain formulas. Polyunsaturated fats replaced many of the saturated fats. This processed food, made tasty by the various companies that cooperated with the study, was offered at regular prices and included more than 90 different products. The men and their families enjoyed this food, and when the project ended, many wanted to know where they could buy

it. The answer was: "Nowhere."

Why? It's a matter of pure economics. No manufacturer wants to prepare special foods unless he can promote their special health-inducing properties. Yet, the federal Food and Drug Administration forbids advertisers to claim that their food lowers blood cholesterol, thus lessening one of the risk factors of heart disease. Many years ago, before adequate study had taken place, such claims might have been premature and misleading. But now, the American Heart Association and many prominent researchers have been pressing the F.D.A. to reject this policy, but so far without success.

Our ignorance of the basic facts of nutrition is certainly reflected in the attitude of many toward the fluoridation of water. What has fluoride and fluoridation to do with nutrition? We now know that fluoride is considered an important mineral nutrient, essential for healthy teeth and strong bones. A 25-year study in Newburgh, N.Y., has shown conclusively that a tiny amount of fluoride added to the city's water supply dramatically reduces dental caries and the premature loss of teeth and eliminates thousands of toothaches. When compared to a nearby town, with approximately the same population but without fluoride in the water, it was shown that tooth decay among Newburgh residents was cut by two-thirds, and the cost of dental care was reduced by more than one-half. And the Newburgh study is only one of dozens that have been done in recent years.

Studies have also shown that lifelong drinking of fluoridated water hardens the bones, making them less susceptible to osteoporosis, a common disease of aging. One recent study has shown that fluoride in the water, in concentrations above that used in fluoridation, prevents the deposition of calcium in the aorta, the body's main artery—in other words, it lessens hardening of the arteries.

The nature-food cult seems to be increasing throughout our country, but this interest has not contributed to better nutrition. The idea behind this movement is that simple, nonprocessed food is the only kind that is good for us. The cultists contend that additives or chemicals added to food are detrimental, if not outright dangerous. Actually, the reverse is true. Americans have profited by the enrichment, or fortification, of certain basic foods. By adding iodine to table salt, for example, we have reduced goiter and could virtually wipe it out if iodized salt was used exclusively. Vitamin D, which has long been added to milk, prevents young children from having rickets. Necessary vitamins are added to margarine and flour. These "chemicals" have not hindered us; rather, they have helped us. Because our nutrition education is so skimpy, most of us have not realized that enrichment and fortification have been a part of food processing for a long time.

Food chemistry is a part of our technological age. Just as certain vitamins and minerals have long been added to the food we eat, so will other needed nutrients be added, such as certain essential amino acids that are low in cereals. Additives to prevent spoilage are also necessary if we are to be sure of getting wholesome food into our kitchens. Without certain preservatives it would be impossible to ship food over long distances. Furthermore, the back-to-the-earth policy, even if it were desirable for a few, is highly impractical as a national policy. It's impossible to embrace such an idea and live in the crowded world of today and tomorrow. If man is going to improve his nutritional health and feed the expanding population, he will have to accept prepared foods containing a variety of additives with the knowledge that they are full of all the nutritive elements he needs.

The new day in food calls for getting used to "chemical additives." All of the body processes are just a matter of chemistry anyway, and we are actually composed of chemicals, just as is our food. New synthetics are not harmful to our body, if they are used correctly. Nor do the other additives we use impair nutri-

tion. In fact, without these additives we would have a much tougher job feeding our population and we probably would have a good bit more malnutrition. It is true that large amounts of certain substances can be harmful, but we haven't used them that way. We must continue to recognize the safe and unsafe ways of using additives.

One can hope for the day when anyone can sit down to a meal at any restaurant, at a Fourth of July picnic or at home and have hot dogs and potato salad and be sure that the food is really nutritious. New answers are being found continuously in the laboratory. We already know much more than we have the courage to apply. The nature-food kick is only a hazardous detour to what promises to be a golden age for nutrition.

Scientific application will come only when we have an informed public. As was shown at the White House Conference on Food, Nutrition and Health last December, there is a demand for technical knowledge and technical application. Consumer groups, medical schools, schools of all levels, even physicians are asking for assistance. We need to mobilize all our resources in order to prevent the hidden hungers—to keep our countrymen from being overfed but undernourished, and to feed the underfed and undernourished.

●　●　●

THE 4 BASIC FOODS

The concept of the "Basic Four" food groups was developed by Harvard's Department of Nutrition, published in the *Journal of the American Dietetic Association* in 1955, and was subsequently adopted by the United States Department of Agriculture. The following is based on the leaflet *Food for Fitness,* issued by the Agriculture Department.

Choose food from these four groups to be sure of getting the proper nutrients needed for good health.

Meat and Meat Substitutes
Beef, lamb, veal, pork, liver, heart, kidney; poultry and eggs; fish and shellfish. *Alternates:*

Group 1: Meat and Meat Substitutes

Group 2:
Milk and Dairy Products

1118

Group 3:
Fruits
and Vegetables

Group 4: Bread and Cereals

Dry beans, peas, lentils, nuts, peanut butter. *Recommended daily:* 2 or more servings a day—lean meat, poultry, fish, liver, eggs. (Where applicable 2-3 oz., cooked, not including bone.) Dry beans, peas, lentils—1 cup, cooked—or peanut butter—4 tablespoons.

Milk and Dairy Products

Milk—fluid, whole, evaporated, skim, dry or buttermilk; cheese—cottage, cheddar-type, natural or processed; ice cream. *Recommended daily:* Milk (8 oz. glasses): Daily quota for children—3-4 glasses; teenagers—4 or more glasses; adults—2 or more glasses. *Substitutes:* Cheese—1-inch cube cheddar = ⅔ cup milk. Cottage cheese—½ cup = ⅓ cup milk. Cream cheese—2 tablespoons = 1 tablespoon milk. Ice cream—½ cup = ¼ cup milk.

Fruits and Vegetables

Vitamin C—good sources: Grapefruit, oranges, strawberries. Fair sources: Honeydew, tangerines, asparagus tips, brussels sprouts, raw cabbage, leafy green vegetables, tomatoes, potatoes. *Recommended daily:* four or more servings daily. (Count as one serving ½ cup of fruit or vegetable.) Vitamin C—one serving daily from "good sources," or two from "fair sources." *Vitamin A:* Dark-green vegetables—broccoli, cress, kale and spinach, turnip greens; deep-yellow vegetables—carrots and pumpkin, sweet potatoes, winter squash; fruits—apricots, cantaloupe. *Recommended daily:* Vitamin A—one serving every other day. Additional servings from any other fruits and vegetables.

Bread and Cereals

Bread, crackers, cereals (cooked and ready-to-eat), cornmeal, grits, macaroni, spaghetti, noodles, rice, rolled oats, baked goods. (Bread and cereals should be whole-grained, enriched, or restored.) *Recommended daily:* four or more servings a day. A serving includes: 1 slice of bread, 1-oz. ready-to-eat cereal, ½ to ¾ cup cooked cereal, cornmeal, grits, macaroni, noodles, rice, spaghetti.

1119

MAJOR-VITAMIN CHART

	What It Does	Major Dietary Sources	National Vitamin Foundation recommended daily allowance for normal nonpregnant adults
VITAMIN A	Important for normal growth in children. Necessary for good vision. Essential for healthy skin, eyes and hair and, in general, for the health of all the epithelial structures of the body.	Largely found in such foods as milk, butter, fortified margarine, eggs, liver, and kidney. The body also makes its own vitamin A from foods containing carotene, e.g. leafy green and yellow vegetables.	3,000—5,000 International Units. Applies when ⅔ of the Vitamin A activity is supplied as carotene, as occurs in the average American diet.
VITAMIN B₁ *(thiamine)*	Necessary for proper function of heart and nervous system. Early signs of deficiency include loss of appetite, constipation, insomnia, irritability. Required to obtain energy from food.	Enriched cereals, enriched breads, fish, lean meat, liver, milk, pork, poultry, dried yeast, whole-grain cereals.	0.4 milligrams per each 1,000 calories. Never less than 0.8 milligrams daily.
VITAMIN B₂ *(riboflavin)*	Necessary for healthy skin. Helps prevent sensitivity of the eyes to light. Essential for building and maintaining body tissues.	Eggs, enriched bread, enriched cereals, leafy green vegetables, lean meats, liver, dried yeast, milk.	0.6 milligrams per each 1,000 calories in the diet. Never less than 1.2 milligrams daily.
VITAMIN B₆ *(includes pyridoxine, pyridoxamine, and pyridoxal)*	Important for healthy teeth and gums, the health of the blood vessels, the red blood cells, and the nervous system.	Wheat germ, vegetables, dried yeast, meat, and whole-grain cereals.	1.5—2.0 milligrams (estimated content of average American diet)
VITAMIN B₁₂ *(cobalamin)*	Helps prevent certain forms of anemia. Contributes to health of nervous system and proper growth in children.	Liver, kidney, milk, salt-water fish, oysters, lean meat, foods of animal origin in general.	2.0—5.0 micrograms
FOLIC ACID *(pteroylglutamic acid)*	Helps prevent certain forms of anemia and is essential for the integrity of the intestinal tract.	Leafy green vegetables, yeast, meats.	0.05—0.1 milligrams of *free* folic acid
PANTOTHENIC ACID	Essential for synthesis of adrenal hormones, the health of the nervous system, and production of antibodies.	Present in all plant and animal tissues.	About 10.0 milligrams
NIACIN *(niacinamide)*	Necessary for converting food to energy. Aids the nervous system. Helps prevent loss of appetite. Prevents pellagra.	Lean meats, liver, dried yeast, enriched cereals, enriched bread, eggs.	7.0—10.0 milligrams (requirement varies with body weight and caloric intake). Assumes that an equal amount of niacin is formed in the body from tryptophan contained in dietary protein.

	What It Does	Major Dietary Sources	National Vitamin Foundation recommended daily allowance for normal nonpregnant adults
BIOTIN	Necessary for integrity of skin and mucous membranes and for health of red blood cells and cardiovascular systems.	Liver, kidney, eggs, and most fresh vegetables.	Requirement unknown. Normally supplied primarily through synthesis by the intestinal flora.
VITAMIN C (ascorbic acid)	Essential for healthy teeth, gums, and bones. Builds strong body cells and blood vessels.	Citrus fruits, berries, tomatoes, cabbage, green vegetables, peppers, new potatoes.	70.0 milligrams
VITAMIN D (including D2 and D)	Necessary for strong teeth and bones. Prevents rickets. Helps utilization of calcium and phosphorus.	Vitamin-D fortified milk, cod-liver oil, salmon, tuna, egg yolk.	400 International Units
VITAMIN E (tocopherols)	Prevents abnormal peroxidation of tissue fats. Essential for integrity of red blood cells.	Vegetable oils, wheat germ, whole-grain cereals, lettuce.	10—30 International Units (requirement varies directly with the unsaturated-fatty-acid content of the diet)
VITAMIN K	Necessary for normal blood clotting.	Leafy vegetables.	Perhaps 0.5 milligrams (normally supplied mainly through synthesis by the intestinal flora)

GOOD NUTRITION FOR GOOD HEALTH

Any item that concerns nutrition makes headlines nowadays—but never has there been so much confusion about this subject.

Almost daily there are conflicting reports about the foods we eat and their relationship to our health. We hear repeatedly that millions of Americans who can afford to eat properly are actually overfed and undernourished—and don't even realize it.

What *is* good nutrition anyway?

Good nutrition is based on a balanced diet low in saturated fat, which over an extended period of time, helps an individual *maintain his proper body weight* in good health. This kind of diet is made up of choices from the basic food groups, with a recommended fat intake restricted to 35 percent of the day's total calories.

Chart Simplifies Nutrition-Watching

Our Good Nutrition chart is divided into the basic food groups (plus an extra table on Sugars, Sweets and Beverages) and gives you

1121

the calorie, vitamin, mineral, saturated- and polyunsaturated-fat content of 100 ordinarily available foods. The chart also includes the amount of dietary cholesterol in as many foods for which figures are available. Compare the figures listed to see which foods provide your family with the best nutrition values. (For information regarding convenience foods, write to the manufacturers.)

Children stand to gain the most from a prudent diet because they can be taught early in life how to protect their health by making the right food choices. But healthy adults can benefit, too. Changing to a balanced, low-saturated-fat diet *right now* can help correct obesity and may lower the risk of premature heart disease (and other diet-associated illnesses) later in life.

We do need some fat to stay healthy. It is a ready source of energy and acts as a carrier for the fat-soluble vitamins A, D, E and K. However, the *kind* of fat eaten has an important bearing on the cholesterol level of the blood, and it is important to understand just what that relationship is.

Cholesterol, a waxy substance used in the body's chemical processes, is required for good health. But, surplus cholesterol tends to cling to the artery walls, causing atherosclerosis. If it completely clogs a coronary artery, the result is a heart attack.

The Fat-Cholesterol Cycle

There are two sources of cholesterol. One is produced naturally by the body every day. The other, dietary cholesterol, is found in some foods—egg yolks, shellfish, some meats and dairy products—a little in some, more in others. The kind of fat we eat has an effect on both kinds of cholesterol because it has been established that "cholesterol can be lowered, or raised, by the total content of the diet and by the ratio of unsaturated to saturated fats," the ideal ratio being 2 to 1.

Fats are identified as saturated, monounsaturated or polyunsaturated.

Saturated fats tend to raise the cholesterol level. (Keeping the intake to 10 percent of the day's total calories is recommended.) Saturated fats are found in foods of animal origin, in fatty meats, hard table spreads, ice cream, whole-milk cheeses, chocolate and hydrogenated fats. Coconut oil and coconut products are high in saturated fat.

Monounsaturated fats neither raise nor lower blood cholesterol and are present mainly in olives and olive oil.

On the other hand, polyunsaturated fats tend to lower the cholesterol level, and it is recommended that they be used to replace a portion of the saturated fat in the diet. Polyunsaturates are found in liquid oils of vegetable origin and in margarines made from those oils—if "liquid oil" is labeled as the first ingredient—and if the margarines are not completely hydrogenated or hardened. Soft margarines are usually rich in polyunsaturates.

Only a doctor can tell you if cholesterol is a special problem for you or anyone in your family. So don't take it upon yourself to eliminate all the saturated fats from your diet. To do so would be impossible anyway, because they are found in many of the foods we need to maintain good health. Instead, be sensible. Train yourself to be more aware of the kinds and amount of fat you are eating.

Serve moderate portions of the lean cuts of beef, lamb and pork, cooked to dispose of saturated fat, and fat-trimmed on the plate, if necessary. Eat shellfish and organ meats in moderation, since they are higher in dietary cholesterol than most red meats, poultry and fish. Eat sparingly, or avoid those foods that are very high in saturated fat. Try to use cooking methods that do not consistently add unnecessary fat to the daily diet.

The American Heart Association recommends a diet pattern that contains more fish, turkey and chicken, and a greater use of spreads made with polyunsaturated fats, whenever possible. It advises you to avoid rich and overly sweet foods. It suggests a balanced diet low in saturated fats, with a caloric intake adjusted to correct obesity, and a dietary cholesterol intake at 300 milligrams, or less, per day.

With continued good health as the goal, good nutrition is worth whatever effort it takes to modify your family's diet. FAMILY CIRCLE'S Good Nutrition chart was designed to help you achieve that goal.

CHARTING GOOD NUTRITION
FAMILY CIRCLE'S LIFETIME GUIDE TO THE NUTRITIVE VALUE OF FOOD

MEAT GROUP

	Measure or Weight	Calories	Protein grams	Fat grams	Fatty Acids/Saturated grams	Fatty Acids/Polyunsaturated (Linoleic) grams	Cholesterol mg.	Carbohydrates grams	Calcium mg.	Iron mg.	Vitamin A I.U.	Vitamin B/Thiamin mg.	Vitamin B/Riboflavin mg.	Vitamin B/Niacin mg.	Vitamin C/Ascorbic Acid mg.
Chicken, broiled, no skin	3 oz.	115	20	3	1	1	50	0	8	1.4	80	0.05	0.16	7.4	—
Cod fillet, poached	3 oz.	89	20	#	#	#	—	0	11	0.45	0	0.07	0.08	2.5	2
Tuna, in oil, drained	3 oz.	170	24	7	2	1	60	0	7	1.6	70	0.04	0.10	10.1	—
Shrimp, canned	3 oz.	100	21	1	—	—	106	1	98	2.6	50	0.01	0.03	1.5	—
Ground beef, lean	3 oz.	185	23	10	5	trace	60	0	10	3.0	20	0.08	0.20	5.1	—
Lamb, roast, lean	3 oz.	156	24	6	4	trace	60	0	11	1.7	—	0.14	0.25	5.3	—
Veal, roast, med. fat	3 oz.	230	23	14	7	trace	77	0	10	2.9	—	0.11	0.26	6.6	—
Pork, roast, lean	3 oz.	219	25	13	4	1	60	0	11	3.2	0	0.91	0.26	5.5	—
Ham, boiled	3 oz.	203	17	15	6	2	60	0	9	2.4	0	0.38	0.14	2.3	—
Bacon, crisp	2 slices	90	5	8	3	1	*	1	2	0.5	0	0.08	0.05	0.8	—
Beef liver, fried	3 oz.	195	23	9	—	—	257	5	9	7.5	45,420	0.23	3.56	14.1	23
Bologna	2 slices	80	3	7	*	#	*	trace	2	0.5	—	0.04	0.06	0.7	—
Frankfurter, 8 per pound	1	170	7	15	*	#	*	1	3	0.8	—	0.08	0.11	1.4	—
Egg	1 large	80	6	6	.2	trace	275	trace	27	1.1	590	0.05	0.15	trace	0
Red kidney beans, cooked	1 cup	230	15	1	—	—	0	42	74	4.6	10	0.13	0.10	1.5	—
Split green peas, cooked	1 cup	290	20	1	—	—	0	52	28	4.2	100	0.37	0.22	2.2	—
Peanut butter	1 tbsp.	95	4	8	2	2	0	3	9	0.3	—	0.02	0.02	2.4	0
Peanuts	¼ cup	210	9	18	4	5	0	7	27	0.8	—	0.11	0.05	6.1	0
Walnuts	¼ cup	198	6	19	1	9	0	5	trace	1.9	95	0.07	0.04	0.2	—
Coconut	¼ cup	112	1	11	10	trace	0	3	4	0.5	0	0.02	0.01	0.2	1

DAIRY FOODS GROUP

	Measure or Weight	Calories	Protein grams	Fat grams	Fatty Acids/Saturated grams	Fatty Acids/Polyunsaturated (Linoleic) grams	Cholesterol mg.	Carbohydrates grams	Calcium mg.	Iron mg.	Vitamin A I.U.	Vitamin B/Thiamin mg.	Vitamin B/Riboflavin mg.	Vitamin B/Niacin mg.	Vitamin C/Ascorbic Acid mg.
Skim milk, non-fat	1 cup	90	9	trace	—	—	7	12	296	0.1	10	0.09	0.44	0.2	2
Whole milk	1 cup	160	9	9	5	trace	27	12	288	0.1	350	0.07	0.41	0.2	2
Buttermilk	1 cup	90	9	trace	—	—	7	12	296	0.1	10	0.10	0.44	0.2	2
Chocolate drink	1 cup	190	8	6	3	trace	*	27	270	0.5	210	0.10	0.40	0.3	3
Evaporated milk, undiluted	1 tbsp.	22	1	1	1	trace	*	1	40	trace	50	trace	0.05	trace	trace
Light cream	1 tbsp.	30	1	3	2	trace	*	1	15	trace	130	trace	0.02	trace	trace
Heavy cream	1 tbsp.	55	trace	6	3	trace	*	1	11	trace	230	trace	0.02	trace	trace
Powdered imit. cream	1 tbsp.	30	trace	3	2	0	#	3	3	trace	trace	—	—	—	—
Pressurized imit. cream	¼ cup	48	trace	4	4	0	#	2	1	—	85	—	0	—	—
Pressurized wh. cream	¼ cup	39	trace	4	2	trace	*	2	17	—	142	—	0.01	—	—
Dairy sour cream	1 tbsp.	25	trace	2	1	trace	*	1	12	trace	100	trace	0.02	trace	trace
Yogurt, part skim milk	1 cup	125	8	4	2	trace	*	13	294	0.1	170	0.10	0.44	0.2	2
Ice milk	½ cup	100	3	4	2	trace	*	15	102	0.05	140	0.04	0.15	0.05	trace
Ice cream, regular	½ cup	120	3	7	4	trace	30	14	97	0.05	295	0.03	0.14	0.05	trace
Baked custard	½ cup	152	7	8	4	1	150a	15	150	0.6	465	0.06	0.25	0.2	trace
Cottage cheese, dry	½ cup	85	17	1	trace	trace	#	3	90	0.4	10	0.03	0.28	0.1	0
Cottage cheese, creamed	½ cup	130	17	5	3	trace	19	4	115	0.35	210	0.04	0.32	0.1	0
Process. Amer. cheese	1 oz.	105	7	9	5	trace	24	1	198	0.3	350	0.01	0.12	trace	0
Cheddar cheese	1 oz.	115	7	9	5	trace	28	1	213	0.3	370	0.01	0.13	trace	0
Cream cheese	1 oz.	107	2	11	6	trace	34	1	17	0.06	437	0.01	0.06	0.03	0

FATS and OILS

	Measure or Weight	Calories	Protein grams	Fat grams	Fatty Acids/Saturated grams	Fatty Acids/Polyunsaturated (Linoleic) grams	Cholesterol mg.	Carbohydrates grams	Calcium mg.	Iron mg.	Vitamin A I.U.	Vitamin B/Thiamin mg.	Vitamin B/Riboflavin mg.	Vitamin B/Niacin mg.	Vitamin C/Ascorbic Acid mg.
Butter	1 tbsp.	100	trace	12	6	trace	36	trace	3	0	470	—	—	—	0
Margarine, regular	1 tbsp.	100	trace	12	2	3	0	trace	3	0	470	—	—	—	0
Margarine, liq. oil	1 tbsp.	100	trace	11	2	4	0	trace	3	0	470	—	—	—	0
Hydro. veg. shortening	1 tbsp.	110	0	13	3	3	0	0	0	0	—	0	0	0	0
Lard	1 tbsp.	115	0	13	5	1	12	0	0	0	0	0	0	0	0
Corn oil	1 tbsp.	125	0	14	1	7	0	0	0	0	—	0	0	0	0
Cottonseed oil	1 tbsp.	125	0	14	4	7	0	0	0	0	—	0	0	0	0
Peanut oil	1 tbsp.	125	0	14	3	4	0	0	0	0	—	0	0	0	0
Mayonnaise	1 tbsp.	100	trace	11	2	6	#	trace	3	0.1	40	trace	0.01	trace	—
French dressing	1 tbsp.	65	trace	6	1	3	0	3	2	0.1	—	—	—	—	—

Symbols: — indicates value unknown, but probably a measurable amount
  * indicates value unknown, but probably a considerable amount
  # indicates value unknown, but probably very little

continued

	Measure or Weight	Calories	Protein grams	Fat grams	Fatty Acids/Saturated grams	Fatty Acids/Polyunsaturated (Linoleic) grams	Cholesterol mg.	Carbohydrates grams	Calcium mg.	Iron mg.	Vitamin A I.U.	Vitamin B/Thiamin mg.	Vitamin B/Riboflavin mg.	Vitamin B/Niacin mg.	Vitamin C/Ascorbic Acid mg.
FRUIT and VEGETABLE GROUP															
Orange juice	½ cup	60	1	trace	—	—	0	15	13	0.1	275	0.11	0.01	0.5	60
Grapefruit	½ med.	45	1	trace	—	—	0	12	19	0.5	10	0.05	0.02	0.2	44
Strawberries	1 cup	55	1	1	—	—	0	13	31	1.5	90	0.04	0.10	1.0	88
Apple	1 med.	70	trace	trace	—	—	0	18	8	0.4	50	0.04	0.02	0.1	3
Banana	1 med.	100	1	trace	—	—	0	26	10	0.8	230	0.06	0.07	0.8	12
Avocado	½ med.	132	2	13	1.4	1	0	4	9	1.4	460	0.09	0.09	1.4	6
Applesauce, no sugar	½ cup	50	trace	trace	—	—	0	13	5	0.6	50	0.03	0.01	1.0	1
Peaches, canned	½ cup	100	trace	trace	—	—	0	26	5	0.4	550	0.01	0.03	0.7	3
Pineapple, crushed	½ cup	97	trace	trace	—	—	0	25	15	0.4	60	0.10	0.03	0.3	9
Raisins	¼ cup	120	1	trace	—	—	0	32	26	1.5	8	0.04	0.03	0.2	1
Cabbage, shredded raw	½ cup	8	trace	trace	—	—	0	2	17	0.1	45	0.02	0.02	0.1	17
Carrot, raw	1 med.	20	1	trace	—	—	0	5	18	0.4	5,500	0.03	0.03	0.3	4
Tomato, raw	1 large	40	2	trace	—	—	0	9	24	0.9	1,640	0.11	0.07	1.3	42
Green beans, cooked	½ cup	15	1	trace	—	—	0	4	32	0.4	340	0.04	0.06	0.3	8
Spinach, cooked	½ cup	20	3	trace	—	—	0	3	83	2.0	7,290	0.07	0.12	0.5	25
Summer squash, cooked	½ cup	15	1	trace	—	—	0	4	26	0.4	410	0.05	0.08	0.8	10
White potato, baked	1 med.	90	3	trace	—	—	0	21	9	0.7	trace	0.10	0.04	1.7	20
Sweet potato, baked	1 med.	155	2	1	—	—	0	36	44	1.0	8,910	0.10	0.07	0.7	24
Peas, canned	½ cup	83	5	trace	—	—	0	16	25	2.1	560	0.11	0.07	1.1	11
Corn, canned	½ cup	85	3	1	—	—	0	20	5	0.5	345	0.03	0.06	1.1	6
BREAD and CEREAL GROUP															
White bread, enriched	1 slice	70	2	1	—	—	#	13	21	0.6	trace	0.06	0.05	0.6	trace
Whole wheat bread	1 slice	65	3	1	—	—	#	14	24	0.8	trace	0.09	0.03	0.8	trace
Oatmeal, cooked	½ cup	65	3	1	—	1	0	12	11	0.7	0	0.09	0.03	0.1	0
Shredded wheat	1	90	2	1	—	—	0	20	11	0.9	0	0.06	0.03	1.1	0
Corn flakes	1 cup	100	2	trace	—	—	0	21	4	0.4	0	0.11	0.02	0.5	0
Sugared corn flakes	1 cup	155	2	trace	—	—	0	36	5	0.4	0	0.16	0.02	0.8	0
Puffed rice	1 cup	60	1	trace	—	—	0	13	3	0.3	0	0.07	0.01	0.7	0
Rice, enriched, cooked	½ cup	112	2	trace	—	—	0	25	10	0.9	0	0.12	0.01	1.1	0
Macaroni, enr., cooked	1 cup	155	5	1	—	—	0	32	8	1.3	0	0.20	0.11	1.5	0
Egg noodles, enriched	½ cup	100	4	1	trace	trace	*	18	8	0.5	55	0.03	0.01	0.3	0
All-purpose flour	1 tbsp.	28	1	trace	—	—	0	6	1	0.2	0	0.03	0.02	0.2	0
Pancake, 4-inch	1	60	2	2	trace	trace	26b	9	27	0.4	30	0.05	0.06	0.4	trace
Saltines	4	50	1	1	—	—	0	8	2	0.1	0	trace	trace	0.1	0
Graham crackers	4	110	2	3	—	—	0	21	11	0.4	0	0.01	0.06	0.4	0
Brownie	1 med.	95	1	6	1	1	36c	10	8	0.4	40	0.04	0.02	0.1	trace
Doughnut	1 med.	105	3	5	—	#	15	22	147	0.7	0	0.12	0.07	1.0	trace
Angelfood cake	1/12	135	3	trace	—	—	0	32	50	0.2	0	trace	0.06	0.1	0
Yellow cake, choc. icing	1/12	366	4	13	4	2	69d	60	68	0.6	160	0.02	0.08	0.2	trace
Apple pie	⅛	306	3	13	4	3	#	45	9	0.4	35	0.03	0.03	0.4	1
Lemon meringue pie	⅛	269	4	10	4	2	103d	40	15	0.5	175	0.04	0.09	0.2	4
SUGARS, SWEETS, and BEVERAGES															
Granulated sugar	1 tbsp.	40	0	0	—	—	0	11	0	trace	0	0	0	0	0
Brown sugar	1 tbsp.	51	0	0	—	—	0	13	12	0.5	0	trace	trace	trace	0
Jelly	1 tbsp.	50	trace	trace	—	—	0	13	4	0.3	trace	trace	0.01	trace	1
Syrup, corn, blend	1 tbsp.	60	0	0	—	—	0	15	9	0.8	0	0	0	0	0
Molasses, light	1 tbsp.	50	—	—	—	—	0	13	33	0.9	—	0.01	0.01	trace	—
Choc. fudge topping	2 tbsp.	125	2	5	3	trace	#	20	48	0.5	60	0.02	0.08	0.2	trace
Milk choc. candy	1 oz.	145	2	9	5	trace	#	16	65	0.3	80	0.02	0.10	0.1	trace
Cola beverage	12 oz.	145	0	0	—	—	0	37	—	—	0	0	0	0	0
Beer	12 oz.	150	1	0	—	—	0	14	18	trace	—	0.01	0.11	2.2	—
Scotch/80 proof	1½ oz.	100	—	—	—	—	0	trace	—	—	—	—	—	—	—

a—if 2-cup whole-milk, 2-egg recipe, making 4
b—if 1-egg recipe making 12
c—if 2-egg recipe
d—if 3-egg recipe

THE MIRACLE MINERAL THAT KEEPS YOU FIT

By John Prutting, M.D., with Pat Curtis

A 33-year old woman sat in her doctor's office feeling very depressed. Her physical complaints were that she felt tired and weak. But what upset her most was that she couldn't remember things the way she used to and felt unable to cope with her household. She had what is sometimes called "housewife blues."

Her doctor listened to her complaints, examined her, went over her chart and questioned her about her diet. A blood test confirmed his suspicions: The woman was suffering from a deficiency of a very important mineral, magnesium.

The doctor gave her magnesium by injection and put her on a high-magnesium diet. Within two weeks her symptoms had cleared. She felt more energetic, she could handle her housework and she could remember names and appointments as well as ever.

This woman's condition—magnesium deficiency—is not unusual. But her doctor's recognition of it is the result of relatively new findings about this important mineral.

Magnesium is essential to many body processes, and yet, till rather recently most people—even doctors—paid little attention to it. Because magnesium regulates vital actions within cells, it affects the health of muscles, nerves, the brain, kidneys, liver and other organs. These normally contain a high concentration of magnesium, and without it, their function is impaired.

Magnesium is especially important as an activator of enzymes through which we use protein and vitamins. It also helps the utilization of potassium. Magnesium starts the chain reaction in the body to metabolize (make use of) food. In fact, many of the nutrients we consume do us no good unless magnesium is present in the proper amount. For example, undernourished hospitalized patients given large doses of thiamin (B$_1$) and other vitamins by injection remained deficient in those same vitamins till magnesium was added to the injections; then the vitamin deficiencies cleared. Similarly, doctors working with children suffering protein-calcium malnutrition have noted that vitamins and minerals do not help these children without the addition of magnesium.

In a way, magnesium is the "control mineral" that keeps the body working. Lack of it can produce many kinds of adverse symptoms that vary from "the blues" to degrees of muscle weakness.

Magnesium deficiency can cause a condition in which the bowel stops functioning (adynamic ileus), causing constipation. Chronic deficiency can contribute to hardening of the arteries. Mental and emotional symptoms can range from mental fatigue and feelings of being unable to cope, through varying degrees of excitability, irritability, agitation, depression and anxiety. Extreme cases exhibit even maniacal behavior, and some have reached total confusion and coma.

Some of the symptoms most frequently seen by doctors involve the muscles and the heart. Muscle cramps, tremors, palpitation, accelerated heartbeat (tachycardia) and irregular heartbeat (fibrillation) are common in magnesium deficiency.

My own interest in magnesium was started many years ago by a patient, a 43-year-old businessman, who was suffering repeated attacks of incapacitating irregular heartbeat. He was in effect, a cardiac cripple. There was no evidence of any of the usual heart diseases, so I knew his trouble was caused by something else.

I treated him with another vital body mineral, potassium, but he improved only slightly. He told me his heart was more likely to fibrillate when he drank liquor. That proved to be an important clue since it was known that alcohol can produce muscle cramps. But, at that time, we were then just beginning to learn that magnesium is important for proper muscle function and that lack of it can cause muscle irritability, or tremors. The heart, after all, is a muscle. Laboratory tests for magnesium were rare, but I was able to persuade a lab to determine the magnesium level in this man's blood. The test showed it to be very low.

My patient's response to magnesium injections and a high-magnesium diet was immediate and dramatic. I also advised him to avoid high-calcium foods (such as cheese) and excess protein. And I suggested he cut out alcohol, at least temporarily, as alcohol depletes body magnesium. My patient has had no trouble with his heart since. He works hard, enjoys water-skiing and dancing and drinks moderately. But he does maintain a high-magnesium diet.

My reason for suggesting the patient avoid excess calcium and protein in his diet may surprise many of you who have been brought up to call these the "building-blocks" of life. Actually, calcium tends to compete in the body with magnesium—the calcium, when excessive, will be absorbed in preference to the magnesium, and magnesium deficiency may result. Magne-

1125

sium is also important to the body's use of protein. The more protein foods you eat, the more magnesium you need. If you don't get the magnesium, you not only may develop a magnesium deficiency—but you also lose much of the benefit you should be getting from the protein. The same with calcium. Also, excess sugar can lower magnesium.

In general, avoiding excess meat, cheese and milk has the additional advantage of lowering cholesterol.

Excessive use of alcohol is often the culprit in magnesium deficiency. In my experience, almost all heavy daily drinkers are low in magnesium. People who habitually start the evening meal with martinis, a cheese appetizer, and go on to steak or hamburger with potatoes and dessert lower their magnesium level dangerously.

Although poor diet and habitual alcohol intake are the commonest causes of magnesium deficiency, there are also certain medical conditions that can bring on slight or even serious deficiency. Diarrhea is one. Also loss of fluids through surgery, congestive heart failure, acute pancreatitis, kidney diseases, diabetes, even excessive perspiration. Also a disease called hypoparathyroidism, which is due to impaired action of small but important glands in the neck behind the thyroid glands. The physician should watch for magnesium deficiency with any of these conditions.

Those who take diuretics—so-called "water pills"—to lose weight are especially susceptible to magnesium loss. So are women who take these pills to alleviate water retention before menstruation. As the water is flushed out of the body, so is the magnesium.

It should be noted, however, that people vary greatly in their tendency to lose magnesium. Some of us are born with an error in metabolism that causes magnesium loss.

There are several ways a doctor discovers magnesium deficiency in a patient. His first clues of course are the patient's own complaints and the observable clinical signs. Certain characteristics are also revealed in his patient's electrocardiogram. Then the magnesium level in the patient's blood can be tested and correlated with the blood proteins and other minerals. Most hospital laboratories and progressive commercial laboratories now do magnesium tests.

For severe cases of magnesium deficiency, intramuscular or intravenous injections are the only way to get magnesium into the body quickly. Some slight absorption of magnesium can be produced through very small doses of magnesium salts—milk of magnesia, citrate of magnesia, and Epsom salts (magnesium sul-

phate). But unfortunately, because they are laxatives, the magnesium is not absorbed to any great extent—and if the salts cause diarrhea, the patient is worse off than before.

Some of my patients ask me about taking magnesium in vitamin-mineral supplements or in those calcium-and-magnesium tablets sold in health-food stores. Unfortunately, the vitamin-mineral supplements contain too little magnesium to do any real good in a deficiency condition—and if the amount were increased, it might produce diarrhea. The calcium-magnesium tablets do not raise appreciably the magnesium level in the blood, probably because the calcium blocks the benefit of the magnesium.

Leaving aside illnesses that call for injections of magnesium, the most satisfactory way to get the magnesium we need is through the diet.

The best food sources of magnesium are nuts (especially almonds) and seeds—sunflower, sesame, caraway, and pumpkin seeds. Wheat germ, wheat bran, oatmeal, corn and cornmeal are excellent. Mothers of young children should be glad to hear that peanut butter is high on the list of magnesium-rich foods.

Other important sources are fresh green vegetables—broccoli, spinach, green beans, Brussels sprouts, beet greens, turnip greens, chard, kale, and so forth. These vegetables should be cooked—or preferably steamed—only a short time and in very little water, for much of the mineral content can be lost in excess cooking water. If you use frozen vegetables, cook them frozen so that any water that results from thawing will be part of the cooking water.

However, the essential dietary factor in keeping your magnesium supply at a healthy level is *balance*. Protein and calcium are essential to the diet, but they deplete magnesium when taken in excess. For an adult, eating large portions of meat or fish more than once a day, and large amounts of cheese regularly is excessive, especially if you neglect the green vegetables in favor of animal products. Seventy percent of us have mismanaged our diets enough to have some degree of magnesium deficiency.

Among the foods high in the miracle mineral magnesium are these shown at right: orange or yellow vegetables like yams; nuts (especially peanuts, peanut butter and almonds—so let the kids tuck into their favorite peanut butter and jelly sandwiches); such fruits as avocados; and breads, particularly rough whole-grain types.

FOODS HIGH IN MAGNESIUM

In milligrams per edible portion of one pound as purchased

ALMONDS, Dried, shelled	1,225	MUSTARD GREENS	
APRICOTS, Dried (25% moisture),		Raw	86
uncooked	281	Frozen	104
AVOCADOS, Raw	153	OATS, Whole-grain	767
BARLEY, Whole-grain	562	OATMEAL OR ROLLED OATS	
BEANS, Dry		Dry form	653
White, raw	771	OKRA	
Red, raw	739	Raw	145
BEANS, Lima		Frozen	240
Baby, raw	304	PEANUTS, Roasted, shelled	794
Baby, frozen	218	PEANUT BUTTER	785
Mature seeds, dry, raw	816	PEAS, Green, young	
BEANS, Snap		Raw	60
Raw	128	Frozen	109
Frozen	95	PEAS, Mature seeds, dry	816
BEET GREENS, Raw	269	PECANS, Shelled	644
BRAZIL NUTS, Shelled	1,021	PIGEON PEAS, Mature seeds, dry	549
BREADS		PISTACHIO NUTS, Shelled	717
Cracked-wheat	159	RAISINS, Seedless (18% moisture)	
Pumpernickel, dark	322	uncooked	159
Whole-wheat	354	RICE, Brown, raw	399
BROCCOLI		RYE, Whole-grain	522
Raw spears	85	RYE FLOUR, Light	331
Frozen	95	SESAME SEEDS, Whole, raw	821
BRUSSELS SPROUTS		SOYBEAN FLOURS	
Raw	121	Full-fat	1,120
Frozen	95	High-fat	1,234
BUCKWHEAT, Whole-grain	1,039	Low-fat	1,311
CASHEW NUTS	1,211	Defatted	1,406
CHARD, Swiss, raw	271	SPINACH	
CHESTNUTS, Fresh	151	Raw	399
COCONUT MEAT, Dried,		Canned	286
unsweetened	408	Frozen	295
COLLARDS, Raw, leaves without		SWEET POTATOES	
stems	176	Raw	114
CORN, Field, whole-grain, raw	667	Dehydrated flakes	454
CORNMEAL, Whole-ground,		TURNIP GREENS, Raw	221
bolted, dry	481	WALNUTS, Black, shelled	862
COWPEAS, Mature seeds, dry	1,043	Persian or English, shelled	594
CRACKERS, Graham	231	WHEAT, Whole-grain	726
DATES, (Natural and dry)		WHEAT FLOURS	
without pits	263	Whole wheat	513
FIGS, Dried	322	Patent, all-purpose	113
FILBERTS, Shelled	835	WHEAT BRAN, Added sugar and	
HICKORY NUTS, Shelled	726	malt extract (breakfast cereal)	1,905
KALE		WHEAT GERM	1,524
Raw	107	WHEAT PRODUCTS (cereals)	
Frozen	141	Wheat and malted barley cereal,	
KOHLRABI, Raw	123	toasted, instant-cooking, dry form	762
LENTILS, Dry	363	WILD RICE, Raw	585
MALT EXTRACT, Dried	635	YEAST, Brewer's, debittered	1,048

*Adapted from "Composition of Foods," Agriculture Handbook
No. 8, Agricultural Research Service, United States Department of Agriculture.*

More magnesium-rich foods to include in each day's menus: broccoli (other dark green vegetables such as beet greens, spinach, collards, kale, kohlrabi, mustard greens and Brussels sprouts are also high in magnesium); and beans, both the fresh and the dried varieties. Carrots, also pictured here, are a good source of vitamin A but not of magnesium.

HOLIDAY

FEASTS

**HOLIDAY FEASTS:
A FESTIVE NEW YEAR'S
BUFFET, A FESTIVE EASTER
FEAST, A BANG-UP
4TH OF JULY BEACH BLAST,
AN OLD FASHIONED
THANKSGIVING, A CONTI-
NENTAL CHRISTMAS BUFFET**

Holidays are for family, friends and feasting—
preferably all three together. These are the
times fondly remembered—the mixture of fine
foods, fun and fellowship. And these are the
days one tries to re-create with each new New
Year's, Easter, July 4th, Thanksgiving or
Christmas.

In the pages that follow, you'll find five menus
for holiday feasting together with the recipes
needed to make each occasion memorable.

1131

*What a way to toast the New Year in, with an elegantly
groaning board centered with Seafood Newburg and
Ribbon Salad bowl. For dessert, Christmas Ice-Cream
Log.*

A FESTIVE NEW YEAR'S BUFFET

ACT I
Holiday Punch Bowl
Sausage Tartlets
Tomatoes Pyrenees

ACT II
Seafood Newburg
Curried Chicken and Vegetables
Fluffy Rice
Ribbon Salad Bowl
Hot Rolls
Christmas Ice Cream Log
Coffee Tea

Holiday Punch Bowl
Watch the excitement when your guests see the "Orange Volcanoes" that fume and bubble around the ruby punch.
Makes 20 punch-cup servings

6 envelopes (⅝-ounce each) instant daiquiri mix
2 cups light rum
1 can (46 ounces) fruit juicy red Hawaiian punch, chilled
1 bottle (28 ounces) quinine water
  ICE MOLD *(recipe follows)*
1 orange, cut in thin slices
  ORANGE VOLCANOES *(recipe follows)*

1 Dissolve daiquiri mix in rum in a medium-size bowl; refrigerate.
2 Party time: Pour rum mixture into punch bowl; add punch and quinine water; carefully slide in ICE MOLD and add orange slices. Place ORANGE VOLCANOES around punch-bowl tray. Decorate with Christmas greens, if you wish.
  ICE MOLD—Fill an 8-cup mold with water; set in freezer for four hours, or overnight. To unmold, let stand at room temperature about 5 minutes, or until ice is movable in mold. Invert onto a cookie sheet and slide carefully into filled punch bowl.
  ORANGE VOLCANOES—Cut a slice from the top of each of 4 large oranges; hollow out, saving fruit for a family treat. Cut tops of oranges in sawtooth design. (This can be done the day before and the oranges wrapped in plastic bags and refrigerated.) Party time: Fill orange shells to within ½ inch of top with water. Place several

small pieces of dry ice (handle with care and use tongs) in each orange shell. As smoke dies down, add several more small pieces of dry ice. *Note:* Dry ice from your local ice company.

●

Sausage Tartlets
Tiny tarts with a savory filling.
Bake shells at 400° for 5 minutes, then at 375° for 15 minutes. Heat at 400° for 10 minutes.
Makes about 5 dozen

1 package piecrust mix
5 brown 'n serve sausages (½ an 8-ounce package)
¼ pound mushrooms, finely chopped
1 small onion, chopped (¼ cup)
1 egg
½ cup milk
½ cup shredded Cheddar cheese
½ teaspoon salt
½ teaspoon leaf marjoram, crumbled
¼ teaspoon pepper

1 Prepare piecrust mix, following label directions. Pinch off small pieces; press into 1¼-inch tartlet pans. If tartlet pans are not available, tiny muffin pans may be used, pressing the piecrust mix about half way up the sides of the cups. Place tartlet pans in a baking pan for ease in handling.
2 Bake in hot oven (400°) 5 minutes. Remove to wire rack.
3 Cut sausages into very thin slices. Brown in a small skillet; remove to paper toweling with a slotted spoon. Sauté mushrooms and onion in pan drippings until just tender.
4 Beat egg slightly in a medium-size bowl; add milk, cheese, salt, marjoram and pepper. Mix well. Fill tartlet shells, dividing sausage slices evenly.
5 Bake in moderate oven (375°) 15 minutes, or until firm. Remove to wire rack. Let stand a few minutes before removing tartlets from pans.
6 Do-ahead note: Place tartlets in foil or plastic boxes; cover firmly; label and freeze.
7 Party day: Place tartlets in baking pan. Heat in hot oven (400°) about 10 minutes, or until piping-hot. Garnish each with a thin slice of stuffed olive, if you wish. Keep hot on hot tray.

Tomatoes Pyrenees

Cherry tomatoes are tossed in garlic-flavored oil and chopped parsley for a quick and colorful treat.
Makes about 4 dozen

1 pint cherry tomatoes
3 tablespoons olive or vegetable oil
1 clove of garlic, minced
¼ cup finely chopped parsley

1 Stem and wash tomatoes; dry on paper toweling.
2 Heat oil with garlic in a skillet. Add tomatoes and parsley; toss gently to coat and heat tomatoes but not to burst skins.
3 Do-ahead note: This may be done early in the day. Cover tomatoes and chill until serving time.
4 Party time: Insert a food pick into each tomato and place on a hot tray, or return to skillet and heat for several minutes.

Seafood Newburg

Succulent seafood, swimming in sherried cream sauce, adds a touch of elegance to any dinner party.
Makes 8 servings

1 lobster (about 1 pound)
OR: 2 packages (7 ounces each) frozen Rock lobster tails, cooked
6 tablespoons (¾ stick) butter or margarine
⅓ cup flour
1½ teaspoons salt
¼ teaspoon cayenne
¼ teaspoon ground nutmeg
1 cup milk
1 cup cream for whipping
3 egg yolks
½ cup dry sherry
1 pound scallops, cooked
1 pound shrimp, cleaned, deveined and cooked
6 cups hot cooked rice

1 Remove meat from lobster or lobster tails, saving shell or tail shells for garnishing platter, if you wish. Cut meat into bite-size pieces; reserve.
2 Melt butter or margarine in a large saucepan; stir in flour, salt, cayenne and nutmeg; cook, stirring constantly, until bubbly. Stir in milk and cream; continue cooking and stirring until sauce

thickens and bubbles 1 minute; remove from heat.
3 Beat egg yolks slightly in a small bowl; stir in sherry. Slowly stir in a generous ½ cup of the hot sauce, then stir back into remaining sauce in pan. Cook slowly, stirring constantly, 1 minute. Fold in scallops, shrimp and lobster. Heat gently about 5 minutes.
4 Do-ahead note: Line top of an 8-cup double boiler with heavy foil. Spoon in seafood mixture; freeze. When frozen, remove foil-wrapped food from double boiler; return to freezer.
5 Party day: Remove foil from frozen seafood mixture and place in top of double boiler; cover. Heat over hot water 1½ to 2 hours, until thawed and bubbly-hot. Serve over hot rice. Garnish platter with reserved shells and parsley sprigs, if you wish.

Curried Chicken and Vegetables

A different curry—tender boneless chicken breasts in an aromatic curried vegetable sauce, served over steaming rice.
Makes 8 servings

4 whole chicken breasts, split (about 12 ounces each)
¼ cup flour (for chicken)
½ teaspoon salt (for chicken)
⅛ teaspoon pepper (for chicken)
¼ cup (½ stick) butter or margarine
1 large onion, chopped (1 cup)
1 green pepper, halved, seeded and diced
1 tablespoon flour (for sauce)
1 teaspoon salt (for sauce)
⅛ teaspoon pepper (for sauce)
2 tablespoons curry powder
1 can (8 ounces) tomatoes
2 envelopes or teaspoons instant chicken broth
2¼ cups water
6 cups hot cooked rice

1 Pull skin from split chicken breasts; bone. Flatten each half by placing between two pieces of wax paper and pounding with the back of a heavy knife or mallet. Cut each half into 2 pieces (fillets).
2 Combine ¼ cup flour, ½ teaspoon salt and ⅛ teaspoon pepper in a plastic bag. Add chicken fillets; shake well to coat.
3 Melt butter or margarine in a large skillet; sauté chicken fillets until brown on both sides. Remove from skillet.
4 Sauté onion and green pepper until almost tender in same skillet. Stir in the 1 tablespoon flour, 1 teaspoon salt, ⅛ teaspoon pepper and curry powder. Add tomatoes, instant chicken broth and water; bring to boiling.

1133

5 Lower heat; simmer, covered, 20 minutes. Remove cover and simmer 5 minutes longer, or until sauce thickens.

6 Return chicken fillets to sauce and cover. Simmer 15 minutes longer, or until chicken is tender.

7 Do-ahead note: Line a 10-cup shallow freezer-to-table baking dish with heavy foil. Arrange chicken in dish and spoon sauce over; wrap; label and freeze. When frozen, remove foil-wrapped food from dish; return to freezer.

8 Party day: Remove food from freezer and peel off foil. Place in same dish. Bake, covered, in moderate oven (350°) 1 hour, or until bubbly-hot. Serve with hot rice.

Ribbon Salad Bowl

This colorful vegetable salad, with its finely chopped greens, is dressed and served (no tossing needed) a section at a time, so it stays crisp and lively to the party's end.
Makes 8 servings

> 1 package (10 ounces) frozen Fordhook lima beans
> 1 package (10 ounces) frozen cut wax beans
> 1 envelope Italian salad-dressing mix
> 1 envelope bleu cheese salad-dressing mix
> 1⅓ cups vegetable oil
> ½ cup vinegar
> ¼ cup water
> 1 small head romaine, finely chopped
> 1 small head iceberg, finely chopped
> 1 package (10 ounces) fresh spinach, finely chopped
> 2 bunches radishes, thinly sliced
> 2 cucumbers, scored and thinly sliced

1 Cook lima beans and wax beans in separate small saucepans, following label directions. Drain and place in a shallow dish in separate mounds.

2 Prepare Italian and bleu cheese salad-dressing mixes together with oil, vinegar and water in a large jar with a screw top. Pour about ½ cup of dressing over hot vegetables.

3 Do-ahead note: Cover and chill vegetables. (You can also prepare greens, radishes and cucumbers and wrap in plastic and chill.)

4 Party time: Layer romaine, iceberg and spinach in a large salad bowl. Arrange radishes, lima beans, cucumber slices and wax beans in rows on top of greens. Pour remaining dressing over salad, just before serving.

Christmas Ice Cream Log

This little beauty doesn't need a special mold. A clean empty juice can will do just fine.
Makes 8 to 10 servings

> 1 quart vanilla ice cream, slightly softened
> ½ cup chopped maraschino cherries
> ½ cup maraschino-cherry juice
> Few drops red food coloring
> 1½ pints lemon sherbet, slightly softened
> ⅓ cup crème de menthe
> 1 cup cream for whipping
> 3 whole red maraschino cherries with stems
> 4 whole candied green cherries

1 Stir chopped cherries, cherry juice and red food coloring quickly into vanilla ice cream in a medium-size bowl. Using back of spoon or rubber scraper, press ice cream evenly around inside of a 46-ounce juice can (about ¾ inch thick). Freeze at least 2 hours, or until firm.

2 Stir crème de menthe quickly into lemon sherbet in a medium-size bowl; spoon into center of can; cover with foil or transparent wrap. Freeze, in an upright position, at least 6 hours, or overnight.

3 Unmold one or two hours before serving. To unmold: Loosen around edge of mold with a sharp knife; dip mold, in an upright position, quickly into a large saucepan of hot water. Invert onto a plate; shake to loosen; remove mold. Turn the log on side. Cover; return to freezer until surface is firm.

4 When ready to serve, beat the cream until stiff in a medium-size bowl. Remove stems from whole cherries; reserve. With a small sharp knife, cut maraschino cherries ¾ of the way down into 6 sections each, to make petals. Cut candied green cherries in half and place one half into the center of each of the 3 cherry flowers. Cut green leaves from the green candied cherries and reserve.

5 Attach a rosette tip to a pastry bag; spoon whipped cream into bag. Press out into rosettes along bottom and sides and top of ice cream log. Garnish with cherry flowers, leaves and stems. To serve, cut into slices.

A FESTIVE EASTER FEAST

Whitecap Appetizer Cup
Cornucopia Ham Glacé
Golden Mustard Sauce   Apple Relish
Triple-Ring Vegetable Platter
Bouquet Salad
Croissants
Almond-Butter Torte   Demitasse

Whitecap Appetizer Cup

A dollop of dill-seasoned cream floats atop beef broth sparked with crisp vegetables for this hot dinner starter.
Makes 8 servings

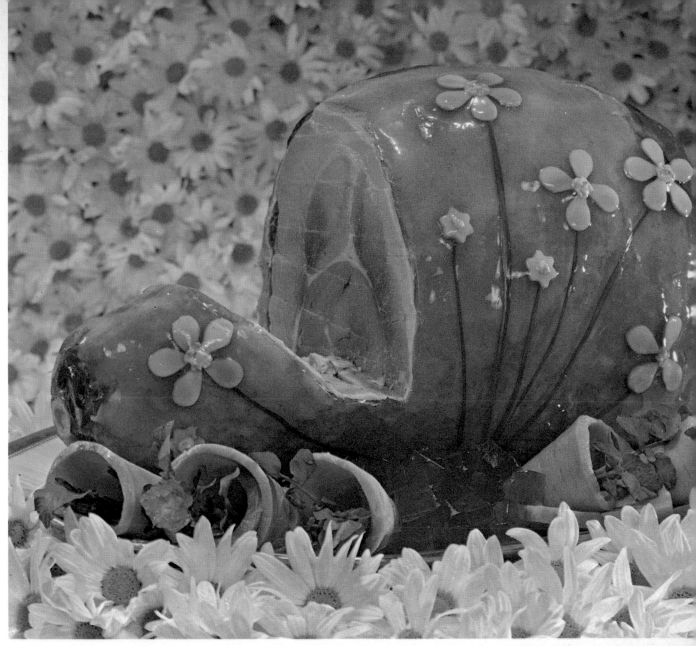

Ham, is for Easter, and what more beautiful than Cornucopia Ham Glacé abloom with egg-onion flowers?

2 cans (10½ ounces each) condensed beef
  broth
2 cups water
½ pound fresh green peas, shelled
½ cup diced pared carrot
½ cup diced celery
  Seasoned pepper
  DILL CREAM (recipe follows)

1 Heat condensed beef broth and water to boiling in a medium-size saucepan; stir in vegetables and a dash of seasoned pepper; cover.
2 Simmer 10 minutes, or until vegetables are crisply tender.

3 Ladle into cups or small soup bowls; float 1 tablespoonful DILL CREAM on each.

DILL CREAM—Season ½ cup dairy sour cream with ¼ teaspoon dillweed and a dash of paprika in a small bowl. Chill 30 minutes to blend flavors. Makes ½ cup.

●

Cornucopia Ham Glacé
You can start this showy star two days ahead. Heating the ham before glazing brings out all of its full rich flavor.
Bake at 325° for 2¼ to 2½ hours. Makes 8

generous servings, plus enough for at least one bonus meal

1 *fully cooked ham, weighing 8 to 10 pounds*
1 *small onion, peeled and sliced*
6 *whole cloves*
6 *peppercorns*
1 *bay leaf*
1 *cup water*
1 *can (about 13 ounces) chicken consommé*
1 *can (about 13 ounces) madrilène*
2 *envelopes unflavored gelatin*
½ *cup apple juice*
1 *green onion*
1 *hard-cooked egg, shelled*
1 *tablespoon soft butter or margarine*
½ *teaspoon prepared mustard*
   Watercress

1 Two days before serving, place ham, fat side up, in a large shallow baking pan.
2 Bake in slow oven (325°) 2¼ to 2½ hours, or until heated through. Chill overnight.
3 The next day, combine onion, cloves, peppercorns, bay leaf and water in a small saucepan; cook 10 minutes. Strain into a medium-size bowl; stir in chicken consommé and madrilène.
4 Soften gelatin in apple juice in a small saucepan; heat over low heat, stirring constantly, until gelatin dissolves; remove from heat. Stir into consommé mixture.
5 Pour 2 cups into a pan, 8x8x2; chill until firm to cube for decorating platter just before serving. Chill remaining gelatin mixture just until as thick as unbeaten egg white.
6 While gelatin chills, cut strips of green onion into different lengths to use for flower stems. Starting at each end of egg, cut very thin rounds of white, then cut rounds into petal and flower shapes with truffle cutters; remove remaining white from yolk to use, if needed. Press yolk through a sieve into a cup; blend in butter or margarine and mustard until smooth.
7 Trim thick skin, if any, from ham (some come without it) and most of the fat layer. Turn ham, meaty side up; cut a thin slice from bottom so ham will stand on platter. Cut a wedge-shape piece from shank end and lift out, then cut 6 thin slices, wrap and chill for making cornucopia garnish.
8 Place ham on a rack in a large shallow pan. Spoon thickened gelatin over top several times to make a thick layer and cover ham completely; chill just until sticky-firm. (Spoon any gelatin mixture that runs into pan back into bowl to use again. To keep gelatin mixture from getting too stiff as you work, set bowl in a pan or lukewarm water.)
9 Arrange green-onion strips and egg-white cutouts in gelatin on ham to form "flowers;"

place a dot of egg-yolk mixture in center of each flower. Carefully spoon another layer of thickened gelatin over all; chill overnight.
10 Just before serving, place ham on a large serving platter; roll saved slices into cornucopias; stuff with watercress. Arrange around ham. Cut chilled gelatin mixture in pan into small cubes; spoon around ham.

Golden Mustard Sauce
Makes 1½ cups

2 *tablespoons butter or margarine*
2 *tablespoons all-purpose flour*
5 *teaspoons dry mustard*
2 *teaspoons sugar*
1 *teaspoon salt*
   Dash of cayenne
1 *cup milk*
2 *egg yolks*
2 *tablespoons cider vinegar*

1 Melt butter or margarine in a medium-size saucepan; stir in flour, mustard, sugar, salt and cayenne. Cook, stirring constantly, just until bubbly. Stir in milk; continue cooking and stirring until sauce thickens and boils 1 minute.
2 Beat egg yolks in a small bowl; stir in a generous ½ cup of the hot mixture, then stir back into remaining sauce in pan. Cook, stirring constantly, 1 minute longer; remove from heat. Stir in vinegar.
3 Serve warm or cold.
Note—Save egg whites to use in making ALMOND-BUTTER TORTE *(recipe follows)*, if you wish.

Apple Relish
Makes 3 cups

3 *medium-size apples, halved and cored*
3 *medium-size dill pickles*
1 *medium-size onion, peeled*
⅓ *cup sugar*
¼ *cup cider vinegar*

1 Put apples, dill pickles and onion through a food chopper, using a coarse blade; place in a medium-size bowl.

2 Stir in sugar and vinegar. Chill at least three to four hours to blend flavors.

●

Triple-Ring Vegetable Platter
Bake at 375° for 45 minutes. Makes 8 servings

16 *small long white potatoes (about 2 pounds),
    pared*
 6 *tablespoons (¾ stick) butter or margarine,
    melted*
 1 *cup grated Swiss cheese (4 ounces)*
½ *cup fine dry bread crumbs*
    Salt and pepper
 2 *packages (9 ounces each) frozen wax
    beans*
 1 *tablespoon chopped parsley*
 2 *packages (10 ounces each) fresh spinach*

1 Parboil potatoes in boiling salted water in a medium-size saucepan 10 minutes; drain.
2 Pour 3 tablespoons of the melted butter or margarine into a pie plate; mix cheese and bread crumbs in a second pie plate. Roll potatoes in butter to coat well, then in cheese mixture to cover completely. Arrange in a single layer in a large shallow baking pan; sprinkle with salt and pepper.
3 Bake in moderate oven (375°) 45 minutes, or until potatoes are tender and golden-brown.
4 While potatoes bake, cook wax beans, following label directions; drain. Season with 2 tablespoons of the remaining butter or margarine and chopped parsley; keep hot.
5 Trim spinach; wash leaves well; drain. Pile into a large saucepan; sprinkle with salt; cover. (No need to add any water.) Steam 5 minutes, or just until leaves wilt; drain well; season with remaining 1 tablespoon butter or margarine
6 When ready to serve, arrange potatoes in a mound in center of a heated large serving platter; spoon beans, then spinach in rings around edge.

●

Bouquet Salad
Makes 8 servings

4 *small stalks Belgian endive*
8 *small radishes*
6 *heads Bibb lettuce*
  Bottled oil-and-vinegar dressing

1 Trim endive, then quarter each lengthwise; make several cuts in each quarter from tip almost to stem end. Place in a bowl of ice and water to crisp and curl.
2 Trim radishes; make 8 deep cuts in each to form petals; place in bowl with endive until opened.

3 Wash Bibb lettuce and dry well; trim cores. Separate leaves and place in a large shallow serving bowl.
4 Drain endive and radishes. Arrange endive, spoke fashion, on top of lettuce in bowl; pile radishes in center. Drizzle with oil-and-vinegar dressing.

●

Almond-Butter Torte
Such a lusciously rich finale for your Easter dinner! Make it ahead, as the meringue layers mellow upon standing.
Bake at 275° for 1 hour. Makes 8 to 10 servings

 1 *can (5 ounces) toasted slivered almonds*
 4 *whole eggs*
 2 *egg whites*
¼ *teaspoon cream of tartar*
 2 *teaspoons vanilla*
1½ *cups sifted granulated sugar*
    COFFEE BUTTER CREAM *(recipe follows)*
1½ *cups cream for whipping*
 2 *tablespoons 10X (confectioners' powdered)
    sugar*

1 Line each of 2 large cookie sheets with a double thickness of brown paper; draw two 8-inch circles on each. (Use an 8-inch round layer-cake pan as a guide.)
2 Chop almonds *very fine.* (Your blender does a quick neat job.) Set aside for Step 4.
3 Separate the 4 eggs, placing whites in a large bowl and yolks in a cup for butter-cream filling. Add the 2 egg whites, cream of tartar, and 1 teaspoon of the vanilla to other egg whites in bowl. (Remaining 1 teaspoon vanilla is for the cream mixture in Step 8.)
4 Beat egg whites until foamy-white and double in volume. Sprinkle in granulated sugar, 1 tablespoon at a time, beating all the time until sugar dissolves completely and meringue stands in firm peaks. (Beating will take about 25 minutes in all with an electric beater.) Fold in chopped almonds.
5 Spoon into the 4 circles on cookie sheets, dividing evenly; spread into thin even rounds with a spatula.
6 Bake in very slow oven (275°) 1 hour, or until firm. Turn off heat and let meringues cool completely in oven. (Overnight is best.)
7 Remove carefully from brown paper with a spatula or long-blade knife.
8 At least 6 hours before serving, make COFFEE BUTTER CREAM. Beat cream with 10X sugar and

1137

remaining 1 teaspoon vanilla until stiff in a medium-size bowl.

9 Place one meringue layer on a large serving plate; spread with one third of the COFFEE BUTTER CREAM and one fourth of the whipped cream mixture. Repeat with remaining layers and fillings, stacking on top of first layer; swirl remaining whipped cream mixture on top. Garnish with more toasted slivered almonds, if you wish. Chill until serving time. Cut into wedges with a sharp, long-blade knife.

Coffee Butter Cream
Makes about 1 cup

4 egg yolks (from meringue layers)
⅓ cup milk
2 tablespoons sugar
1 teaspoon instant coffee powder
¾ cup (1½ sticks) butter or margarine

1 Beat egg yolks slightly in the top of a small double boiler; beat in milk and sugar.
2 Cook, stirring constantly, over simmering water 10 minutes, or until custard thickens and coats a metal spoon; remove from heat. Stir in instant coffee powder; cool completely.
3 Beat butter or margarine until very soft and creamy in a medium-size bowl of electric mixer; beat in cooled custard, 1 tablespoon at a time, beating well after each addition, until mixture is creamy-thick.

A BANG-UP 4th OF JULY BEACH BLAST

1139

Stuffed Chicken Napoli
Chili Spoonburgers
Garden Potato Salad
Calico Vegetable Crunch
Your Favorite Green Salad
French Bread
Sugar Crunch Squares
Brown-Eyed Susans
Fresh Fruit Basket
Pitcher Punch

Everybody out of the water! It's time for a picnic lunch on the sand: Stuffed Chicken Napoli, Chili Spoonburgers, Garden Potato Salad, Calico Vegetable Crunch, punch.

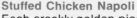

Stuffed Chicken Napoli

Each crackly golden piece hides a zippy salami stuffing for a different flavor.
Makes 8 servings

8 chicken drumsticks with thighs (about 5 pounds)
1 piece (4 ounces) salami
½ cup sifted all-purpose flour
2 teaspoons salt
1 teaspoon paprika
1 teaspoon leaf oregano, crumbled
⅛ teaspoon pepper
½ cup vegetable oil

1 Cut through chicken legs at joints to separate drum sticks and thighs, then cut an opening along bone of each drumstick and in meaty part of each thigh with a sharp knife to make a pocket for stuffing.
2 Cut salami into 16 strips; stuff 1 strip into each piece of chicken.
3 Shake pieces, a few at a time, in mixture of flour, salt, paprika, oregano and pepper in a paper bag to coat evenly.
4 Cook pieces slowly in vegetable oil in a large frying pan 20 minutes; turn; cover loosely. Cook 20 minutes longer, or until tender and crisply golden. Serve warm or cold.
Note—Pack pieces in a large shallow pan lined with paper toweling. Cover tightly.

Chili Spoonburgers
Makes 8 servings

2 pounds ground beef
1 large onion, chopped (1 cup)
1 cup thinly sliced celery
1 can (about 1 pound) stewed tomatoes
1 can (12 or 16 ounces) whole-kernel corn
1 can (4½ ounces) chopped ripe olives
¾ cup bottled chili sauce
2 teaspoons salt
2 teaspoons garlic salt
¼ teaspoon pepper
1 bay leaf
16 split hamburger buns, buttered

1 Shape ground beef into a large patty in a kettle or Dutch oven. Brown 5 minutes on each side, then break up into chunks. Stir in onion and celery; cook, stirring several times, 5 minutes longer.
2 Stir in tomatoes, corn and liquid, olives, chili sauce, salt, garlic salt, pepper and bay leaf;

cover. Simmer 15 minutes to blend flavors. Remove bay leaf. Spoon onto split hamburger buns.
Note—Carry meat mixture in its kettle to reheat on grill at your eating spot. Or, if you're not taking a grill, cover kettle tightly and wrap in several thicknesses of newspaper. Food will stay hot for at least 30 minutes.

Garden Potato Salad
Makes 8 servings

6 medium-size potatoes, pared and diced
2 packages (10 ounces each) frozen lima beans
½ pound sliced bacon
1 tablespoon sugar
1½ teaspoons salt
¼ teaspoon pepper
3 tablespoons cider vinegar
3 tablespoons water
1 cup sliced radishes

1 Cook potatoes, covered, with frozen lima beans in boiling salted water in a large saucepan 10 minutes, or until both vegetables are tender; drain. Place in a large bowl.
2 Cut bacon slices crosswise into quarters. Sauté until crisp in a medium-size frying pan; remove and drain on paper toweling.
3 Pour all drippings from frying pan, then measure 3 tablespoonfuls and return to pan; stir in sugar, salt, pepper, vinegar and water; heat to boiling. Pour over vegetables; toss lightly to mix. Just before serving, arrange radish slices, overlapping, around top; mound bacon in center.
Note—To carry to your picnic, bundle cooked bacon and sliced radishes in separate plastic bags, ready to arrange atop salad just before serving.

Calico Vegetable Crunch
Makes 8 servings

2 cups thinly sliced yellow squash
2 cups thinly sliced zucchini
2 cups diced green pepper
1 pint cherry tomatoes, stemmed and halved
½ cup bottled herb-and-garlic French dressing
1 teaspoon salt

Combine vegetables in a large bowl or plastic container; drizzle with dressing and sprinkle with salt. Toss lightly until vegetables are evenly coated.

Note: If your eating spot is more than 30 minutes away, place dressing in a separate container for easy carrying and toss vegetables with dressing just before serving.

●

Brown-Eyed Susans

Bake at 400° for 8 minutes. Makes 2 dozen large cookies

 5 cups sifted all-purpose flour
 1 teaspoon baking powder
 ¼ teaspoon salt
1½ cups (3 sticks) butter or margarine
 2 cups granulated sugar
 3 eggs
 2 teaspoons grated lemon rind
 2 tablespoons lemon juice
 ½ cup semisweet-chocolate pieces
 Yellow decorating sugar

1 Sift flour, baking powder and salt onto wax paper.
2 Cream butter or margarine with granulated sugar until fluffy-light in a large bowl; beat in eggs, 1 at a time, until well blended; stir in lemon rind and lemon juice.
3 Stir in flour mixture, a third at a time, blending well to make a stiff dough. Chill at least an hour, or until dough is firm enough to handle. (Overnight is even better.)
4 Roll, 3 tablespoonfuls at a time, into balls between palms of hands. Place, 3 inches apart, on greased large cookie sheets. To flatten cookies and shape petals easily: Use your shortening or coffee can with plastic lid attached. Grease lid and dip in additional granulated sugar, then press balls of dough to ¼-inch thickness. Push edge of dough in slightly every 1½ inches with fingertip.
5 Press 3 semisweet-chocolate pieces in center of each round; sprinkle generously with yellow sugar.
6 Bake in hot oven (400°) 8 minutes, or until firm and lightly browned around edges. Remove from cookie sheets with a spatula; let cool completely on wire racks.
Note: Pack cookies in a sturdy box lined with crumpled wax paper or transparent wrap.

Pitcher Punch

Makes 8 servings, about 1 cup each

1 can (6 ounces) frozen concentrate for Hawaiian punch, thawed
1 bottle (32 ounces) apple juice

1 cup water
 Ice cubes

Mix concentrated punch, apple juice and water in a large pitcher. Pour over ice cubes in tall glasses.
Note: Mix beverage at home and carry in a keep-cold jug. Or carry punch and apple juice in their containers, ready for mixing at your picnic spot.

●

Sugar-Crunch Squares

Bake at 350° for 40 minutes. Makes one 13x9x2-inch loaf

Cake
3⅜ cups sifted all-purpose flour
4½ teaspoons baking powder
 1 teaspoon salt
 ¾ cup (1½ sticks) butter or margarine
1½ cups sugar
 2 eggs
1½ teaspoons vanilla
 1 cup z 2 tablespoons milk
Topping
 ¾ cup sifted all-purpose flour
 ¾ cup firmly packed light brown sugar
 ½ teaspoon cinnamon
 Pinch of cloves
 ⅓ cup butter or margarine
 1 cup chopped walnuts or pecans
 10X (confectioners' powdered) sugar (decoration)

1 Make cake: Sift flour, baking powder and salt onto wax paper.
2 Cream butter or margarine with sugar until fluffy in a medium-size bowl; beat in eggs and vanilla.
3 Blend in dry ingredients, alternately with milk, just until smooth. Pour into a greased baking pan, 13x9x2.
4 Bake in a moderate oven (350°) 25 minutes; remove from oven. (Leave heat on.)
5 Make topping while cake bakes: Combine flour, sugar and spices in a small bowl; cut in butter or margarine until mixture is crumbly. Stir in nuts.
6 Sprinkle over partly baked cake; return to oven at once and bake 15 minutes longer or until golden on top and cake springs back when lightly pressed with fingertip.
7 Cool at least 5 minutes on wire rack. To decorate, lay 1-inch strips of wax paper or foil across top of cake, on the diagonal and about 1-inch apart. Dust 10X sugar over cake. Remove paper strips. To serve, cut in large squares.

1141

AN OLD-FASHIONED THANKSGIVING

Lobster Bisque with Wheat Crackers
Roast Ribs of Beef
Holiday Roast Turkey
Scalloped Oyster Stuffing   Giblet Gravy
Golden Potato Cones   Yam Puff
Browned Onions in Squash Boats
Green Beans Parisienne
Lime Relish Baskets
Whitecap Cranberry Crown
Parker House Rolls

Lobster Bisque
Makes 8 servings

2 *cans (about 6 ounces each) lobster meat*
1 *medium-size onion, chopped (½ cup)*
¾ *cup (1½ sticks) butter or margarine*
¾ *cup sifted all-purpose flour*
2 *cans (10½ ounces each) condensed chicken broth*
¾ *cup dry sherry*
3 *cups light cream or table cream*
2 *tablespoons tomato paste (from a 6-ounce can)*
½ *teaspoon salt*
 Dash of pepper

1 Drain lobster; remove any bony tissue. Set aside several large pieces for garnish, then dice remainder.
2 Sauté onion in butter or margarine until soft in a large saucepan; stir in flour. Cook, stirring constantly, until bubbly.
3 Stir in chicken broth; continue cooking and stirring until mixture thickens and boils 1 minute. Stir in diced lobster and sherry; cover; simmer 20 minutes.
4 Blend in cream, tomato paste, salt and pepper; heat *slowly* just until hot. Ladle into a tureen; float saved pieces of lobster on top. Serve with wheat crackers, if you wish.

1143

Holiday Roast Turkey
Roast at 325° about 4 hours

For 8 servings, plus some left for another meal, buy a turkey weighing about 12 pounds.
 If you buy a regular fresh or frozen turkey, follow directions below for thawing, if needed, stuffing and roasting.

Just the proper Thanksgiving mood, just the proper food.

To thaw: Keep bird in its original wrapper and store in your refrigerator, allowing from 2 to 3 days. Remove giblets and neck from body or neck cavity; wash and cook for GIBLET GRAVY *(recipe follows).* Rinse inside of turkey with cold water; drain well. Store, lightly covered, in refrigerator until ready to stuff and roast.

To stuff: Make SCALLOPED OYSTER STUFFING *(recipe follows),* but do not put into bird until just before roasting time. Sprinkle inside of bird lightly with plain or seasoned salt, then lightly stuff neck cavity. Smooth neck skin over stuffing and skewer to back of bird. Twist wing tips until they rest flat against skewered neck skin. Next stuff body cavity. If your turkey comes "tucked," slide legs out, stuff bird lightly, then slip legs back in place. If your turkey is not a "tucked" type, lace opening together with poultry pins or skewers and string and truss legs close to body.

To roast: Brush stuffed bird all over with melted butter or margarine. (You'll need about 6 tablespoons [¾ stick].) Place, breast side up, in roasting pan—on a rack, if you wish—but do not add water or cover pan. If using a meat thermometer, stick bulb into the center of a thigh without touching bone. Roast in slow oven (325°) for time suggested on turkey wrapper, or about 4 hours for an about-12-pounder, or until thermometer registers 185°. After bird has been in the oven about 30 minutes, brush again with melted butter. During rest of roasting time, baste every half hour with buttery drippings in pan.

To test for doneness: Start testing 30 minutes before roasting time is up. Protecting your fingers with paper toweling, squeeze meaty part of thigh. It should feel soft. Now move drumstick up and down. It should twist and move easily. When turkey is done, place it on a heated platter and keep warm while making gravy. (Turkey slices more easily and neatly if allowed to stand for 15 to 20 minutes.) Garnish platter with chicory or curly endive and LIME RELISH BASKETS *(recipe follows).* Carve bird and serve.

1144

Scalloped Oyster Stuffing
Makes about 10 cups or enough to stuff a 12-pound turkey.

1 medium-size onion, diced (½ cup)
1 cup thinly sliced celery
1 cup (2 sticks) butter or margarine
2 cans (8 ounces each) oysters
1 cup light cream or table cream
¼ cup chopped parsley
½ teaspoon salt
¼ teaspoon pepper
3 packages (3½ ounces each) unsalted soda crackers, coarsely crushed

1 Sauté onion and celery in butter or margarine until soft in a small saucepan; remove from heat.
2 Drain liquid from oysters into onion mixture; stir in cream, parsley, salt and pepper.
3 Combine oysters and crackers in a large bowl; drizzle onion mixture over top; toss lightly to mix. Let stand about 5 minutes, or until liquid is absorbed. Cover and chill until ready to stuff into turkey.

Giblet Gravy
Makes about 4 cups

Combine turkey giblets (except liver) and neck with 1 medium-size onion, chopped; a few celery tops; 1 teaspoon salt; 1 bay leaf; and 4 cups water in a medium-size saucepan; cover. Simmer 1 hour and 40 minutes; add liver. Simmer 20 minutes longer, or until meat is tender. Strain broth; measure; add water, if needed, to make 4 cups. Chop giblets fine and stir into broth. Cool, then chill until ready to make gravy. After turkey has been removed from roasting pan, remove rack, if used; tip pan and let fat rise in one corner. Pour all fat into a cup, leaving juices in pan. Measure 8 tablespoons fat and return to pan; blend in ½ cup flour. Cook, stirring constantly, just until bubbly. Stir in the 4 cups broth and giblets. Continue cooking and stirring, scraping baked-on juices from bottom and sides of pan, until gravy thickens and boils 1 minute. Season to taste with salt and pepper; stir in a little bottled gravy coloring to darken, if you wish.

Golden Potato Cones
Makes 8 servings

Instant mashed potatoes
Butter or margarine
Salt
Water
2 eggs, separated
½ cup sifted all-purpose flour
1 cup sliced blanched almonds
Vegetable shortening or vegetable oil for frying

1 Prepare 4 cups instant mashed potatoes with butter or margarine, salt and water in a large saucepan, following label directions and omitting milk; beat in egg yolks. Divide into 8 even mounds; shape each into a cone.
2 Beat egg whites slightly in a pie plate; spread flour and almonds on separate pieces of wax paper.
3 Carefully roll each potato cone in flour, then in beaten egg white and almonds; stand on a plate; chill.
4 Melt enough vegetable shortening or pour vegetable oil into a large frying pan to fill two-thirds full; heat to 360°.
5 Fry potato cones, two or three at a time, turning once, 2 minutes, or until golden. Lift out with a slotted pancake turner; drain on paper toweling. Serve hot.
Note—Potatoes may be fried several hours ahead, if you wish. Just before serving, place on a cookie sheet. Reheat in slow oven (325°) 20 minutes.

⬤

Yam Puff
Bake at 325° for 1 hour and 10 minutes. Makes 8 servings

6 large yams or sweet potatoes
4 eggs, separated
4 tablespoons (½ stick) butter or margarine
1 cup light cream or table cream
3 tablespoons sugar
1 tablespoon grated orange peel
½ teaspoon ground cinnamon
¼ teaspoon ground nutmeg

1 Cook yams or sweet potatoes in boiling salted water in a large saucepan 30 minutes, or until tender; drain. Cool until easy to handle, then peel; place in a large bowl.
2 While potatoes cool, beat egg whites until they stand in firm peaks in a medium-size bowl.
3 Break up potatoes with a fork, then beat in egg yolks, butter or margarine, cream, sugar, orange peel, cinnamon and nutmeg; continue beating until fluffy-light. Fold in beaten egg whites. Spoon into a greased 8-cup baking dish.
4 Bake in slow oven (325°) 1 hour and 10 minutes, or until slightly puffed and firm. Garnish with orange slices, if you wish.

⬤

Browned Onions in Squash Boats
Makes 8 servings

4 tablespoons (½ stick) butter or margarine
2 tablespoons vegetable oil
40 small white onions (about 2 pounds), peeled
2 envelopes instant beef broth

OR: 2 beef-flavor bouillon cubes
1 teaspoon dried parsley flakes
¼ teaspoon garlic powder
¼ teaspoon leaf thyme, crumbled
1 cup water
STEAMED SQUASH *(recipe follows)*

1 Melt butter or margarine with vegetable oil in a large frying pan; stir in onions. Sauté, turning often, 10 minutes, or until golden.
2 Stir in beef broth, parsley, garlic powder, thyme and water; heat to boiling; cover. Simmer 30 minutes, or until tender.
3 Spoon onions and sauce into STEAMED QUASH. Sprinkle onions with paprika, if desired.
STEAMED SQUASH—Trim 4 small acorn squashes; halve each lengthwise; scoop out seeds. Place halves, cut sides down, in two large frying pans; pour boiling water into each pan to a depth of ½ inch; cover. Steam 30 minutes, or until squashes are tender; drain. Brush hollows with melted butter or margarine.

⬤

Lime Relish Baskets
Makes 8 servings

8 large limes
1 jar (6 ounces) marinated artichoke hearts
1 can (12 or 16 ounces) whole-kernel corn, drained
1 can or jar (4 ounces) pimientos, drained and diced
1 tablespoon grated onion
2 tablespoons sugar
¼ teaspoon salt

1 Make lime baskets this way: Mark a guideline lengthwise around center of lime with the tip of a knife, then mark off a ¼-inch-wide strip across the top for handle. Cut out sections between marks and remove remaining lime pulp from bottom. Wrap baskets in foil or transparent wrap and chill.
2 Dice enough of the lime pulp to measure ¼ cup; place in a medium-size bowl. (Use remainder for punch or for flavoring fruit cup.) Drain liquid from artichoke hearts into bowl with lime; chop artichokes and add with corn, pimientos, onion, sugar and salt; toss lightly to mix. Chill at least 6 hours to season.
3 When ready to serve, trim a thin slice from bottom of each lime basket, if needed, to make basket stand flat; spoon corn mixture into baskets.

1145

Green Beans Parisienne
Makes 8 servings

3 packages (9 ounces each) frozen cut green beans
1 cup thinly sliced celery
4 tablespoons (½ stick) butter or margarine
¼ cup water
1 teaspoon salt
4 medium-size mushrooms, trimmed and sliced

1 Combine green beans, celery, butter or margarine, water and salt in a medium-size frying pan. Heat to boiling; cover.
2 Cook 8 minutes; add mushrooms. Cook 2 minutes longer, or just until beans are tender.
3 Spoon into a heated serving bowl; drizzle buttery sauce from pan over top.

Whitecap Cranberry Crown
Makes 8 servings

4 envelopes unflavored gelatin
1 bottle (48 ounces) cranberry-apple drink
¼ cup mayonnaise or salad dressing
¼ cup dairy sour cream
3 ripe pears, pared, quartered, cored, and diced
Watercress

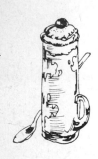

1 Soften gelatin in 2 cups of the cranberry-apple drink in a medium-size saucepan. Heat slowly, stirring constantly, until gelatin dissolves; remove from heat. Stir in remaining 4 cups cranberry-apple drink.
2 Measure ½ cup of the gelatin mixture into a small bowl; set aside. Chill remaining gelatin mixture 50 minutes, or until as thick as unbeaten egg white.
3 Beat mayonnaise or salad dressing and sour cream into the ½-cup gelatin mixture; pour into an 8-cup tube mold.
4 Place mold in a pan of ice and water to speed setting; chill just until sticky-firm.
5 Fold pears into thickened gelatin mixture in saucepan; carefully spoon over dressing layer in mold. Remove from ice and water. Chill in refrigerator at least 6 hours, or overnight.
6 When ready to unmold, run a sharp-tip, thin-blade knife around top of salad, then dip mold *very quickly* in and out of hot water. Cover mold with a large serving plate; turn upside down, then gently lift off mold. Garnish center of salad and plate with watercress.

1146

A CONTINENTAL CHRISTMAS BUFFET

MENU

Festive Pâté en Croûte
Celery Hearts   Olives
Herbed Beef Roast
Crown Roast of Pork
Vegetable Bouquet Platter
Swiss Scalloped Potatoes
Cucumber-Lime Cream Mold
Hot Croissants   Butter Balls
Christmas Green Mint Pie
Old English Trifle
Fruits in Snow
Cream Mints   Salted Nuts
Coffee

Festive Pâté en Croûte
Bake at 325° for 1½ hours, then at 425° for 45 minutes. Makes 8 to 12 servings

½ pound sliced bacon
1 pound chicken livers
¼ cup sifted all-purpose flour
2 teaspoons salt
½ teaspoon pepper
1 teaspoon leaf thyme, crumbled
4 tablespoons light cream or table cream
3 tablespoons Cognac
1½ pounds ground veal
1 pound ground pork
2 eggs
PÂTÉ PASTRY (recipe follows)

1 Line the bottom and sides of an 8¼-inch pâté mold or a 9x5x3-inch loaf pan with bacon slices.
2 Place half of the chicken livers in an electric blender container. Whirl until smooth, about 1 minute. Add remaining chicken livers and whirl again until smooth.
3 Add flour, salt, pepper, thyme, cream and Cognac to chicken livers and blend until smooth. (If you don't have a blender, put chicken livers through a food grinder, using the fine blade, then stir in other ingredients in a medium-size bowl.)
4 Mix ground veal and pork together until smooth in a large bowl. Beat eggs in a small bowl, reserving 2 tablespoons for Step 10. Beat remaining beaten egg and the liver mixture into ground meats to make a very smooth mixture. Pour all but 1 cup of meat mixture into prepared mold. Chill remaining cup of mixture for Step 8. Top meat mixture in mold with remaining bacon strips. Place mold in a shallow baking pan.
5 Bake in slow oven (325°) 1½ hours; remove

Guaranteed to kindle the Christmas spirit in every Scrooge, a buffet with a showy Crown Roast of Pork.

from oven. Cool in mold on a wire rack, placing a heavy dish over pâté to weigh it down. When cool, remove weight, then slip pins off sides of mold; remove mold from pâté. For loaf pan, turn pâté out of pan; remove all bacon strips. (Pâté mixture may be prepared to this step, then refrigerated, one or two days ahead.)

6 Wash, dry and grease the sides of mold; slip pins into place and place mold on a shallow baking pan. (Or line a 9x5x3-inch loaf pan with foil, leaving a 1-inch overhang on all sides; grease foil.

7 Roll out ⅔ of PATÉ PASTRY to a 18x 14-inch

oval on a lightly floured pastry cloth or board. Fold pastry in half and fit into bottom and up sides of pâté mold. (Or roll out pastry to a 16x12-rectangle for loaf pan.)

8 Fit baked pâté into pastry-lined mold, loosening pins on sides of mold for ease of fitting; tighten pins into place. Spread cooked pâté with reserved meat mixture.

9 Roll out remaining PATÉ PASTRY to an 11x7-inch oval. Using pâté mold base as a guide, cut a top crust; make slits in center of crust; place on top of pâté. (Or roll out pastry to 10x6-inch rectangle for loaf pan.)

10 Beat reserved 2 tablespoons egg with 2 tablespoons of water in a cup. Brush pastry with egg wash.

11 Trim pastry overhang to ½ inch; turn edge up, flush with rim; press into top crust. Make pastry decorations with trims, using tiny hors d'oeuvres cutters; brush with egg wash.

12 Bake in hot oven (425°) 30 minutes. Remove from oven and remove pâté-mold sides. Brush top and sides of pastry with egg wash; cover top crust with aluminum foil. (Or lift pâté out of loaf pan, using overhanging foil as lifters, then remove foil.)

13 Bake in hot oven (425°) 15 minutes longer, or until pastry is golden. Serve warm or cold.

Pâté Pastry
Makes crust and trims for 1 pâté

   3½ cups sifted all-purpose flour
     1 teaspoon salt
     1 cup (2 sticks) butter or margarine
     2 eggs, beaten
     3 tablespoons ice water

1 Sift flour and salt into a large bowl. Cut in butter or margarine until crumbly with a pastry blender.

2 Make a well in center of mixture and add beaten eggs and water. Stir with a fork to make a stiff pastry.

3 Turn out onto a lightly floured pastry cloth or board and knead 10 times. Wrap in foil or plastic wrap and chill at least 2 hours.

Herbed Beef Roast
Roast at 325° for 3 hours. Makes 8 servings

   1 rolled boned rib roast of beef, weighing about 8 pounds
  ½ cup unsifted all-purpose flour
   4 tablespoons leaf rosemary, crumbled
   2 tablespoons dry mustard
   2 tablespoons seasoned salt
   2 teaspoons seasoned pepper

1 Preheat oven to slow (325°).

2 Wipe roast with wet paper toweling, leaving surface very moist.

3 Combine flour, rosemary, mustard, seasoned salt and seasoned pepper in a small bowl. Sprinkle evenly over moist surface of meat, patting on firmly with palms of hands.

1148

4 Place roast, fat side up, on rack in shallow roasting pan; do not add water or cover pan. Insert meat thermometer into roast so the bulb end reaches the center of the meat and does not rest in fat.

5 Roast 3 hours, or until thermometer registers 140°—rare; or 160°—medium.

6 Remove meat from oven; place on a heated serving platter. Cover loosely with foil; let stand 20 minutes in a warm place. (This makes roast easier to slice.) Turn roast meat side up. Carve across the grain, cutting strings as you carve.

Crown Roast of Pork
Roast at 325° for 3 hours. Makes 8 servings

   1 sixteen- to eighteen-chop crown pork roast
   1 large onion, chopped (1 cup)
   1 cup chopped celery
   6 tablespoons (¾ stick) butter or margarine
   1 can (6 ounces) frozen orange juice concentrate, thawed
   4 cups cubed white bread (8 slices)
   1 teaspoon salt
  ¼ teaspoon fennel seed, crushed
  ⅛ teaspoon pepper
   1 pound cranberries, washed and stemmed
  ½ cup honey
     Preserved kumquats
     Watercress
     CRANBERRY ORANGE CUPS (recipe follows)

1 Preheat oven to slow (325°).

2 Place roast, rib ends up, on a piece of foil in a shallow roasting pan. Wrap ends of bones with foil. Insert meat thermometer into roast so bulb end reaches the center of one chop without touching bone.

3 Roast 2 hours, or until thermometer registers 160°.

4 While roast cooks, sauté onions and celery in butter or margarine until soft in a medium-size skillet. Stir in ¼ cup of the orange juice concentrate; heat mixture to boiling; pour over bread cubes in a medium-size bowl. Add salt, fennel and pepper; toss lightly until evenly moist. Stir in 1 cup of the cranberries.

5 Spoon stuffing lightly into hollow center of roast, mounding slightly. Continue roasting pork for another 30 minutes.

6 Blend remaining orange juice with honey in a small saucepan; heat to boiling; reduce heat; simmer 2 minutes. Brush outside of roast with part of the orange mixture. Continue roasting, brushing several times with remaining orange mixture, 30 minutes, or until thermometer registers 170° and pork is tender and richly glazed.

7 Lift roast onto a heated large serving platter; remove foil. Garnish rib ends with kumquats.

Frame roast with watercress and CRANBERRY ORANGE CUPS.

8 Carve between ribs into servings.

CRANBERRY ORANGE CUPS—Cut 4 small seedless oranges in half. With a small sharp knife, scallop the cut edge, then scoop out centers to make a cup. Chop centers. Heat 1½ cups sugar and 1½ cups water to boiling in a medium-size saucepan. Add chopped orange and remaining 3 cups cranberries. Cook, following label directions; cool; fill orange cups. Serve any remaining cranberry sauce separately.

Vegetable Bouquet Platter
Makes 8 servings

1 large head cauliflower (about 3 pounds)
2 packages (about 9 ounces each) frozen cut green beans
2 cans (14 ounces each) small whole carrots
⅓ cup butter or margarine
2 tablespoons finely chopped parsley
1 tablespoon lemon juice
Dash of salt

1 Trim outer green leaves from cauliflower, but leave head whole. Cook, covered, in boiling salted water in a large saucepan 30 minutes, until crisply tender.

2 While cauliflower cooks, heat carrots with their juice until bubbly in a medium-size saucepan. Cook green beans in a medium-size saucepan, following label directions.

3 Lift cauliflower from saucepan with a two-tined fork; place in center of a large heated serving platter. Drain carrots and green beans. With a slotted spoon, arrange around cauliflower.

4 Melt butter or margarine in a small saucepan; add parsley, lemon juice and salt. Pour over vegetables.

Cucumber-Lime Cream Mold
Makes 8 servings

3 packages (3 ounces each) lime-flavored gelatin

1½ teaspoons salt
2⅔ cups boiling water
2 tablespoons cider vinegar
3 cups dairy sour cream (1½ pints)
2 medium-size cucumbers, pared and finely chopped (2 cups)
⅔ cup chopped green onion

1 Dissolve gelatin and salt in boiling water in a large bowl. Stir in vinegar. Chill until as thick as unbeaten egg white.

2 Beat in sour cream; fold in cucumbers and onion. Pour into an 8-cup mold. Chill about 4 hours, or until firm.

3 Just before serving, loosen salad around edge with a knife; dip mold *very quickly* in and out of hot water. Wipe water off mold. Shake mold gently to loosen. Cover with a serving plate; turn upside down; gently lift off mold. Garnish with tiny lettuce leaves, cherry tomatoes and cucumber slices, if you wish.

Swiss Scalloped Potatoes
Bake at 325° for 1 hour and 45 minutes. Makes 8 servings

3 pounds of potatoes, pared and thinly sliced (8 cups)
1 medium onion, grated
½ pound Swiss cheese, grated
3 eggs
2¼ cups milk
2 teaspoons salt
¼ teaspoon pepper
½ teaspoon paprika

1 Heat 3 quarts of water to boiling in a kettle; add potatoes. Cook, uncovered, 5 minutes; drain.

2 Place alternating layers of potatoes, onion and cheese in a buttered 12-cup shallow baking dish.

3 Combine eggs, milk, salt and pepper in a small bowl; beat well. Pour over potatoes. Sprinkle top with paprika. Cover baking dish with foil.

4 Bake in slow oven (325°) for 45 minutes. Remove foil; continue baking 1 hour longer, or until golden-brown.

Christmas Green Mint Pie
Bake at 325° for 10 minutes, then at 450° for 4 minutes. Makes 8 servings

1 package (5 ounces) shortbread cookies, crushed (about 1⅓ cups)
½ cup finely chopped pecans
⅓ cup firmly packed light brown sugar

6 tablespoons (¾ stick) butter or margarine, melted
½ cup water
10 tablespoons granulated sugar
2 tablespoons green crème de menthe
1 quart vanilla ice cream, softened
½ cup cream for whipping
    Few drops green food coloring
3 egg whites
⅛ teaspoon cream of tartar

1 Blend shortbread crumbs, pecans, brown sugar and butter or margarine in a medium-size bowl. Press mixture firmly over bottom and side of a 9-inch pie plate.
2 Bake in slow oven (325°) 10 minutes, or until set. Cool completely on a wire rack.
3 Combine water with 4 tablespoons of the sugar in a small saucepan; cover. Bring to boiling; uncover; continue boiling, without stirring, 7 minutes. Remove from heat; cool slightly; stir in crème de menthe; cool completely.
4 Spread half the ice cream in an even layer in cooled pie shell; cover; freeze until firm.
5 Combine cream with food coloring in a small bowl; beat until stiff. Fold in 2 tablespoons of the cooled crème de menthe syrup into the cream. Spread evenly over firm ice cream in pie shell. Freeze until firm. Top with remaining ice cream. Freeze until firm. Pie may be wrapped in foil or plastic wrap, and kept frozen for a week before the buffet.
6 Beat egg whites with cream of tartar until foamy-white and double in volume in a medium-size bowl. Beat in the remaining 6 tablespoons sugar, 1 tablespoon at a time, until meringue stands in firm peaks. Pile meringue onto filling, sealing firmly to crust edge and swirling into peaks. Freeze overnight.

7 Just before serving, brown meringue until lightly golden in very hot oven (450°) for 4 minutes. Drizzle with remaining crème de menthe syrup; serve at once.

1150

Old English Trifle
Makes 8 servings

6 egg yolks
½ cup sugar
2¼ cups milk
2 cups cream for whipping
¼ cup cream sherry
2 baker's jelly rolls (about 11 ounces each)
    Red candied pineapple or red candied cherries
    Angelica or citron

1 Beat yolks slightly with sugar in the top of a double boiler. Stir in milk and 1 cup of the cream.
2 Cook, stirring constantly, over simmering water, 25 minutes, or until mixture is thickened and coats a spoon.
3 Strain custard into a medium-size bowl; cool slightly; stir in sherry.
4 Cut each jelly roll into 6 slices and line a pretty crystal serving bowl. Pour warm custard carefully over slices; cover bowl with foil or transparent wrap. Chill thoroughly, 3 hours or more.
5 To serve: Beat remaining 1 cup cream until stiff in a small bowl. Decorate top of trifle with poufs of cream. Garnish with slivers of candied pineapple or cherries and angelica or citron.

Fruits in Snow
This is an edible centerpiece.

9 apples, various varieties and sizes
5 pears, various varieties and sizes
3 oranges
2 large bunches purple grapes
2 large bunches green grapes
2 lemons
2 limes
    Strawberries
    Kumquats
2 egg whites, lightly beaten
4 cups VANILLA SUGAR (recipe follows)
    Lemon leaves

1 Wash and dry fruits on paper toweling. Brush each piece of fruit with egg white, then sprinkle generously with VANILLA SUGAR. Allow to dry on cookie sheets. (You can place the grapes on cookie sheets, brush with egg white, and sprinkle with sugar.)
2 When ready to assemble, choose a three-tiered stand. Arrange bunches of grapes over edge of stand and place a large piece of fruit over grapes to keep them in place.
Arrange alternating colors and shapes of large fruit on stand to make a pretty composition. Place groups of strawberries and kumquats in spots for color accents. Garnish with lemon leaves.

VANILLA SUGAR—Scrape the seeds from a 4-inch length of vanilla bean. (You will find vanilla bean in a jar in the spice section of the supermarket.) Stir into 4 cups granulated sugar in a jar. Place the pod in the jar, too; cover, and let stand about a week to develop the full flavor.

INDEX TO RECIPES IN THIS VOLUME